The Letters
of Joe Hill

The Letters of Joe Hill
Centenary Anniversary Edition

*Compiled and edited, with historical notes
on the famous Wobbly songwriter*

by Philip S. Foner
with new material by Alexis Buss

Haymarket Books
Chicago, Illinois

Originally published as *The Letters of Joe Hill*, compiled and edited by Philip S. Foner. Oak Publications, 1965.

This expanded edition features Joe Hill's pre-prison writings and his songs, accompanied by editorial notes, as well as new and significantly revised comments on letters that Hill wrote in prison. Those comments are marked with the initials "AB."

Photograph of Buster Flynn (p. 62) and "My Last Will" (p. 69) courtesy of the Tamiment Library, New York University.

Images of letters to Katie Phar (pp. 10, 20–21, 31, 32–33) reproduced courtesy of the Rare Book & Manuscript Library, University of Illinois at Urbana-Champaign.

Photograph of Katie Phar (p. 25) reproduced courtesy of University of Washington Library, Digital Collections.

Postcards to Charles Rudberg (pp. 17, 77, 78) reproduced courtesy of the Archives of Urban & Labor Affairs, Wayne State University.

Telegram from Joe Hill to W. A. F. Ekengren (p. 61) reproduced courtesy of Swedish National Archives, Stockholm.

Images from *Industrial Worker, Industrial Pioneer, Solidarity*, and *One Big Union Monthly* reproduced courtesy of Industrial Workers of the World, www.iww.org.

This edition published in 2015 by
Haymarket Books
P.O. Box 180165
Chicago, IL 60618
773-583-7884
www.haymarketbooks.org
info@haymarketbooks.org

ISBN: 978-1-60846-497-5

Trade distribution:
In the US, Consortium Book Sales and Distribution, www.cbsd.com
In Canada, Publishers Group Canada, www.pgcbooks.ca
In the UK, Turnaround Publisher Services, www.turnaround-uk.com
All other countries, Publishers Group Worldwide, www.pgw.com

This book was published with the generous support of Lannan Foundation and Wallace Action Fund.

Cover design by John Yates.

Library of Congress Cataloging-in-Publication data is available.

Entered into digital printing November, 2022.

☙ TABLE OF CONTENTS ❧

➢ FOREWORD ≈
BY TOM MORELLO

Joe Hill is my favorite musician, though there are no known recordings of him. Joe was The O. G. Punk Rocker, the poet laureate of the working class in the early twentieth century. Joe Hill invented the political protest song for the modern age and was a tireless crusader for justice through his music and his union, the Industrial Workers of the World.

Joe was a brilliant satirical lyricist who fearlessly skewered the oppressors of his day with wit and fire. The issues Hill tackled were not much different than those we face today: extreme poverty, police brutality, economic injustice, criminalized immigration, militarism, racism, threats to freedom of speech, war. "The world ain't gonna change itself, that's up to you," was the message of Joe's music. But Joe didn't just sing songs confronting injustice. He was on the front lines risking life and limb to try to create a better, more just world. That's why the powers that be were so afraid of him. That's why they killed him.

Itinerant worker, singer, fighter, badass. Enlightening and inspiring, Joe Hill's influence is everywhere. Without Joe Hill, there's no Woody Guthrie, no Dylan, no Springsteen, no Clash, no Public Enemy, no Minor Threat, no System of a Down, no Rage Against the Machine. On tour in northern Sweden, I visited the tiny room in the house where Joe Hill and his family of nine grew up. The place houses a union headquarters now and has union guards round the clock because fascists regularly try to burn the place down. Why? Because one hundred years after his death, they're still afraid of him. And for good reason. Some of Joe's ashes are buried beneath a tree on the property. I sat under that tree and sang "I Dreamed I Saw Joe Hill Last Night" because, ya see, as the song says, Joe Hill ain't dead. Wherever, whenever you raise your voice, your fist, or your guitar in the name of justice and freedom, Joe Hill is right there by your side.

Solid.

⤞ INTRODUCTION ⤝
BY PHILIP S. FONER

In July 1937, when the Industrial Workers of the World (IWW) was only a shell of an organization, the *One Big Union Monthly*, its official organ, wrote: "One of the things the working-class movement is indebted to the IWW for is the teaching of the value of songs in the struggle for emancipation." And to no other IWW songwriter is the working class more indebted than to Joe Hill, the Wobblies' most famous and most prolific writer of working-class songs.

Joe Hill was born Joel Hägglund in Gävle, Sweden, on October 7, 1879. His father was a conductor on the Gävle-Dala railroad, a low-paying job. Both parents were talented in music, and the father, to interest the children in music at an early age, built an organ by hand. Joel had a violin, an accordion, and a guitar at home, but preferred the violin, playing the instrument mostly by heart.

Joel's father died when he was only eight years old, and four years later Joel began to work for a living, first as a rope maker, later as a fireman in a wood refining factory, and more frequently, at odd jobs. Often sick, he found it difficult to continue working for long periods. During these intervals he occupied himself with his interests in music—composing and playing. His first songs were rewrites of hymns, but none of them seem to have had any political or labor content; they were mostly what his sister called "teasing songs."

Joel's mother died in 1902 and, after selling the family house, he and his brother Paul left for America. For ten years Joel worked at many jobs; during this time he changed his name to Joseph Hillstrom and became popularly known as Joe Hill. He stacked wheat and laid pipe; he cleaned spittoons in a Bowery saloon; he dug copper and shipped it out; he worked on docks and in smelters. And he wrote poems, songs, bits of verse, all kinds of things. In 1910, Joe Hill joined the IWW local in San Pedro, California. A year later, while working as a dock-walloper in San Pedro, he wrote his first known song, "Casey Jones—the Union Scab," a parody of the original Casey Jones song which had appeared two years before. Written to assist the workers on strike on the South Pacific

1

Line who were faced with defeat by the importation of scabs, the song was an immediate success. Printed on colored cards which were sold to assist the strike fund, the song helped keep the strike alive. Within a few months it was being sung by workers in many parts of the country, as migratory laborers carried it across the land.

During the next three years Joe Hill became one of the leading contributors to the IWW's "Little Red Songbook," and by 1913 he was the most popular of the little band of poets and songwriters—including Richard Brazier, Ralph Chaplin, Laura Payne Emerson, Covington Hall, James Connell, and Charles Ashleigh—whose works appeared in the pages of the songbook. The "Preacher and the Slave," "Where the Fraser River Flows," "John Golden and the Lawrence Strike," "Mr. Block," "Scissor Bill," "What We Want," and "The Tramp" were some of the songs by Joe Hill that became famous as soon as they were published. As their titles reveal, Joe Hill's songs emerged out of the actual conditions and struggles of the workers, were consciously written to be used as weapons, and were sung on numerous picket lines during the heyday of the IWW. In her tribute to Joe Hill as a songwriter, published in the May 22, 1915, issue of *Solidarity*, Elizabeth Gurley Flynn wrote:

> Joe writes songs that sing, that lilt and laugh and sparkle, that kindle the fires of revolt in the most crushed spirit and quicken the desire for fuller life in the most humble slave. He has put into words the inarticulate craving of "the sailor, and the tailor and the lumberjack" for freedom; nor does he forget "the pretty girl that's making curls." He has expressed the manifold phrases of our propaganda from the gay of "Mr. Block" and "Casey Jones" to the grave of "Should a gun I ever shoulder, 'tis to crush the tyrant's might." He has crystallized the organization's spirit into imperishable forms, songs of the people—folk songs.

Elizabeth Gurley Flynn's article was written just after she had visited Joe Hill in prison in Salt Lake City where he was awaiting execution. He had been convicted of the slaying, on January 10, 1914, of John G. Morrison, a Salt Lake City grocer. The conviction was based on the flimsiest of evidence—all circumstantial—after a trial conducted in an atmosphere of hatred for the IWW organizer. Joe Hill's lawyers summed up the situation aptly when they wrote in *Solidarity* on May 23, 1914: "The main thing the state has against Hill is that he is an IWW and therefore sure to be guilty."

It is unnecessary here to discuss the various aspects of the case of Joe Hill. But much of what is important is set forth in his letter to the Utah Board of Pardons, September 28, 1915, and the reader would do well to turn to that letter first. While not all of the points in the letter can be fully substantiated, the main ones are sound. The letter, moreover, is especially significant since Hill based much of his defense on the records of the preliminary hearings and the testimonies of the state's witnesses at the trial. Both of these records have disappeared from the office of the responsible authorities in Salt Lake County. Since Hill cited testimony from the recorded transcripts which clearly proved that the leading witnesses against him had changed their testimony between the preliminary hearing and the trial, it appears obvious that a real effort had been made to "fix" the case against him. It would seem that his statements would have been challenged or denied by the press, the Supreme Court of Utah judges, counsel for the State, Governor William Spry, or some other official. But no one bothered to comment on Hill's letter. To have done so would only bring Hill's charge to wider public attention.

However, the Swedish Minister to the United States did read Hill's letter to the Pardon Board, and, his interest aroused by the quotations from the record, he wrote to Judge Morris L. Ritchie (who had presided at the trial), asking for a complete record of the testimony given before the court. The request was turned down. Minister W. A. F. Ekengren, however, obtained the transcript of the preliminary hearings and the trial court from O. N. Hilton, Hill's lawyer. After he had read them, he announced his firm belief that Joe Hill had not had a fair trial and that the evidence against him should never have resulted in a conviction. He appealed to Governor Spry for a commuted sentence.

Thousands of Americans and other thousands abroad were convinced that Joe Hill told the truth when he affirmed that he had nothing to do with the murder and that he was the victim of a frame-up. So they joined in an international defense movement urging that the conviction be reversed or that Joe Hill be granted a new trial. At its 1915 convention, the American Federation of Labor unanimously adopted a resolution which pointed out that "Joseph Hillstrom, a workingman of the State of Utah, and active in the cause of labor" had been sentenced to be shot, that "the grounds for this conviction and sentence appear to be utterly inadequate ..., and that the rights of said Joseph Hillstrom do not appear to have been sufficiently, or at all safeguarded, but on the contrary seem to have been violated to such an extent that the said Joseph Hillstrom did not have a fair and impartial trial. . . ." The resolution, in the name of the A.F. of L., urged the Governor of Utah "to exercise his prerogative of clemency in this case, and to stop the execution of the said Joseph Hillstrom, and that he be given a new and fair trial."

By the spring and summer of 1915, the defense movement had grown to such proportions that President Woodrow Wilson twice asked Governor Spry for "justice and...a thorough reconsideration of the case of Joseph Hillstrom." But the state authorities of Utah, fearing the rising militancy and organization of the workers for whom Joe Hill was an inspiring spokesman, decided that he had to die. On November 19, 1915, Joe Hill was executed, shot with four dum-dum bullets.

At Joe Hill's funeral procession in Chicago, 30,000 people marched, and a news reporter asked: "What kind of man is this whose death is celebrated with songs of revolt, and who has at his bier more mourners than any prince or potentate?" Joe Hill's letters answer this question. All written during his imprisonment, they show him as a class-conscious worker who concerned himself first and foremost, even while facing execution, with the problems confronting the American working class in its struggles against hunger and want. They show him as a man who was ready to sacrifice his life for what he regarded as a sacred principle—the right of a working man to a fair trial. They show him as a man who was convinced that, regardless of what might be his own fate, the cause to which he had devoted the major part of his life—the emancipation of the working class—would ultimately triumph.

THE LETTERS OF JOE HILL

WRITTEN WHILE INCARCERATED IN SALT LAKE CITY, UTAH

The following is the first known letter from Joe Hill while he was in prison. There were likely others before it. By the time he penned this note to E. W. Vanderleith, who was an active Wobbly and a prolific writer for the IWW press, Hill had been incarcerated for 233 days. He was arrested on January 14, 1914. His trial began on June 10, and on July 8, he was sentenced to death with an execution date of September 4, 1914. —AB

SALT LAKE COUNTY JAIL
SEPTEMBER 4, 1914

E. W. VANDERLEITH
SAN FRANCISCO, CALIFORNIA

Dear Friend and Fellow Worker:

Well, Van, this is Sept. 4 which was supposed to be my last day on earth—but I am still wriggling my old lead pencil and I might live a long time yet, if I don't die from "Beanasitis" (that's a brand new disease).

I was up before Hisonor Sept. 1st. My attorney, Soren X. Christensen, made a motion to postpone all proceedings until Judge Hilton arrived from the East. The motion was denied. Then he had to make the argument alone right then and there. He made a pretty good argument although he was not prepared for it.

Among other things he pointed out the fact that no human being can tell by the smell if a gun loaded with smokeless powder has been shot one year, one month, one hour or ten minutes before examination, as our expert had testified; but the "Court" proved by the European war news that the soldiers smelled on the guns in Brussels to find out if they had been recently shot. And in the face of such proofs Christensen had to shut up like a clam. What else could he do, Van? What else could anybody do?

Well, I was denied a new trial on account of them countrymen of yours going round smelling the end of guns and then sending telegrams about it. Well, I don't wish them anything bad but—I hope they'll all choke themselves with sauerkraut.

Well, Van, all joking aside, I guess I have a long wait ahead of me and I think the best you all can do is to forget me for awhile. I know you would do anything for me, Van, and I will never forget the untiring fellowship that you boys showed me during my trial. I don't thank you for it and I make no promises but I'll always remember it. But the best you boys can do is to forget me and use your energies and your financial resources for the One Big Union.

I think some of you are making too much fuss about me anyway. I wish you would tell those who are writing poems about me that there is no poetry about my personality. I am just one of the rank and file—just a common Pacific Coast wharf-rat—that's all. I have always tried to be true to my friends and to my class. What any outsider may think about me is no concern of mine.

7

How THE MEMORY DOTH LINGER.

A RECOLLECTION—Sam Murray as a Mexican Revolutionist, Drawn by Joe Hill.

This portrait of Sam Murray by Joe Hill was published posthumously in the December 1923 *Industrial Pioneer*.

SALT LAKE COUNTY JAIL
SEPTEMBER 15, 1914

SAM MURRAY

Dear Friend and Fellow Worker

Yours of Sept 9 at hand. Glad to hear you are still alive and kicking and back on the firing line again.

So, you tried to imitate Knowles, the Nature Freak, and live the simple life. It might be all right for a little while, as you say, but I am afraid a fellow would get "simple" of getting too much of the simple life.

Well, I guess the wholesale butchery going on in Europe is putting the kibosh on everything, even the organization work, to some extent. As a rule, a fellow don't bother his head much about unions and theories of the class struggle when his belly is flapping up against his spine. Getting the wrinkles out is then the main issue and everything else, side-issued. That's human nature or animal instinct rather, and any amount of soapboxing will not change it. The man who coined the phrase "War is hell" certainly knew what he was talking about. Well, Sam, old boy, I guess Van has told you everything about my case and I think he knows more about it than I do, because he has been around here and on the outside. I am feeling well under the circumstances and I am fortunate enough to have the ability to entertain myself and to look at everything from the bright side. So there is nothing you could do for me, Sam. I know you would if you could.

Well, with best wishes to the bunch in Frisco, I remain, Yours for the OBU
Joe Hill

P.S. Is Jack Mosby in Washington yet or did he leave?

Joe Hill met Sam Murray for the first time in 1911 when he joined IWWs in Baja California, Mexico, to help overthrow Mexico's longtime dictator, Porfirio Diaz. The IWW army was led by John R. Mosby.

World War I had broken out in Europe in August 1914.

Like many Wobblies, Joe Hill addressed most of his correspondents as Fellow Worker (often abbreviated as "F.W.") and ended most of his letters, "Yours for the O.B.U." (the One Big Union).

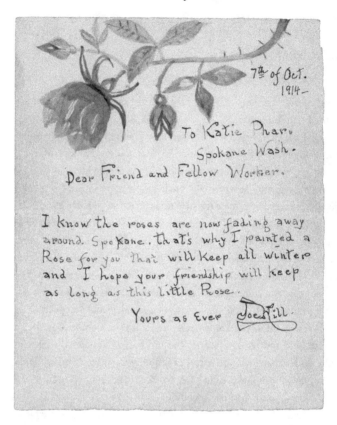

SALT LAKE COUNTY JAIL
OCTOBER 7, 1914

KATIE PHAR
SPOKANE, WASHINGTON

Dear Friend and Fellow Worker:

I know the roses are now fading away around Spokane and that's why I painted a Rose for you that will keep all winter and I hope your friendship will keep as long as this little Rose.

Yours as ever, Joe Hill

Katie Phar (1905–1943) was the ten-year-old daughter of an IWW member in Spokane, Washington. Known as the "IWW Songbird," she led an IWW children's choir and served as song leader at the Spokane IWW hall. —AB

SALT LAKE COUNTY JAIL
NOVEMBER 29, 1914

Editor, Solidarity:

I see in the "Sol" that you are going to issue another edition of the Song Book, and I made a few changes and corrections which I think should improve the book a little, which I am enclosing herewith.

Now, I am well aware of the fact that there are lots of prominent rebels who argued that satire and songs are out of place in a labor organization and I will admit that songs are not necessary for the cause; and whenever I "get the hunch" I intend to make some more foolish songs, although I realize that the class struggle is a very serious thing.

A pamphlet, no matter how good, is never read more than once, but a song is learned by heart and repeated over and over; and I maintain that if a person can put a few cold, common sense facts into a song, and dress them (the facts) up in a cloak of humor to take the dryness off of them, he will succeed in reaching a great number of workers who are too unintelligent or too indifferent to read a pamphlet or an editorial on economic science.

There is one thing that is necessary in order to hold the old members and to get the would-be members interested in the class struggle and that is entertainment. The rebels of Sweden have realized that fact, and they have their blowouts regularly every week. And on account of that they have succeeded in organizing the female workers more extensively than any other nation in the world. The female workers are sadly neglected in the United States, especially on the West coast, and consequently we have created a kind of one-legged, freakish animal of a union, and our dances and blowouts are kind of stale and unnatural on account of being too much of a "buck" affair; they are too lacking the life and inspiration which the woman alone can produce.

The idea is to establish a kind of social feeling of good fellowship between the male and female workers, that would give them a little foretaste of our future society and make them more interested in the class struggle and the overthrow of the old system of corruption. I think it would be a very good idea to use our female organizers, Gurley Flynn, for instance, *exclusively* for the building up of a strong organization among the female workers. They are more exploited than the men, and John Bull is willing to testify to the fact that they are not lacking in militant and revolutionary spirit.

By following the example of our Swedish fellow workers, and paying a little more attention to entertainment with original song and original stunts and pictures, we shall succeed in attracting and interesting more of the young blood, both male and female, in the One Big Union.

Yours for a change,
Joe Hill
Address Jos. Hillstrom, Co. Jail, Salt Lake City, Utah

The IWW began putting out the "Little Red Songbook" in 1909, and the edition Joe Hill refers to was the eighth. Hill sent along additions and changes for some of his songs for this edition, but the material arrived too late to be added. The editor promised: "Will keep them on file for a later edition."

"Gurley Flynn" was Elizabeth Gurley Flynn, the IWW's outstanding woman organizer, who was to play a leading role in the defense of Joe Hill.

SALT LAKE COUNTY JAIL
DECEMBER 1914

How to Make Work for the Unemployed

Much has been written lately about various new ways and tactics of carrying on the class struggle to emancipate the workers from wage slavery.

Some writers propose to "organize with the unemployed"; that is to feed and house them in order to keep them from taking the jobs away from the employed workers. Others again want to organize a Gunmen Defense Fund to purchase machine guns and high powered rifles for all union men, miners especially, that they may protect themselves from the murderous onslaughts of the private armies of the master class. Very well; these tactics MAY be perfectly good, but the question arises: Who is going to pay for all this?

Estimating the unemployed army to be about five millions in number and the board bill of one individual to be five dollars a week, we find that the total board bill of the whole unemployed army would be twenty-five million dollars per week.

The price of a machine gun is about $600 and a modern high-power rifle costs from $20 to $30. By doing a little figuring we find that fifty million dollars would not be sufficient to buy arms for the miners, let alone the rest of the organized workers. Every workingman and woman knows that, after all the bills are paid on pay day, there is not much left to feed the unemployed army or to buy war supplies with.

What the working class needs today is an inexpensive method by which to fight the powerful capitalist class and they have just such a weapon in their own hands.

This weapon is without expense to the working class and if intelligently and systematically used, it will not only reduce the profits of the exploiters, but also create more work for the wage earners. If thoroughly understood and used more extensively it may entirely eliminate the unemployed army, the army used by the employing class to keep the workers in submission and slavery.

In order to illustrate the efficacy of this new method of warfare, I will cite a little incident. Some time ago the writer was working in a big lumber yard on the west coast. On the coast nearly all the work around the water fronts and lumber yards is temporary.

When a boat comes in a large number of men are hired and when the boat is unloaded these men are "laid off." Consequently it is to the interest of the workers "to make the job last" as long as possible.

The writer and three others got orders to load up five box cars with shingles. When we commenced the work we found, to our surprise, that every shingle bundle had been cut open. That is, the little strip of sheet iron that holds the shingles tightly together in a bundle had been cut with a knife or a pair of shears, on every bundle in the pile—about three thousand bundles in all.

When the boss came around we notified him about the accident and, after exhausting his supply of profanity, he ordered us to get the shingle press and re-bundle the whole batch. It took the four of us ten whole days to put that shingle pile into shape again. And our wages for that time, at the rate of 32¢ per hour, amounted to $134.00. By adding the loss on account of delay in shipment, the "holding money" for the five box cars, etc., we found that the company's profits for that day had been reduced by about $300.

So there you are. In less than half an hour's time somebody had created ten days' work for four men who would have been otherwise unemployed, and at the same time cut a big chunk off the boss's profit. No lives were lost, no property was destroyed, there were no law suits, nothing that would drain the resources of the organized workers. But there WERE results. That's all.

This same method of fighting can be used in a thousand different ways by the skilled mechanic or machine hand as well as by the common laborer. This weapon is always at the finger tips of the worker, employed or unemployed.

If every worker would devote ten or fifteen minutes every day to the interests of himself and his class, after devoting eight hours or more to the interests of his employer, it would not be long before the unemployed army would be a thing of the past and the profit of the bosses would melt away so fast that they would not be able to afford to hire professional man-killers to murder the workers and their families in a case of strike.

The best way to strike, however, is to "strike on the job." First present your demands to the boss. If he should refuse to grant them, don't walk out and give the scabs a chance to take your places. No, just go back to work as though nothing had happened and try the new method of warfare.

When things begin to happen be careful not to "fix the blame" on any certain individual unless that individual is an "undesirable" from a working class point of view.

The boss will soon find that the cheapest way out of it is to grant your demands. This is not mere theory; it has been successfully tried more than once to the writer's personal knowledge.

Striking on the job is a science and should be taught as such. It is extremely interesting on account of its many possibilities. It develops mental keenness and inventive genius in the working class and is the only known antidote for the infamous "Taylor System."

The aim of the "Taylor System" seems to be to work one-half of the workers to death and starve the other half to death. The strike on the job will give every worker a chance to make an honest living. It will enable us to take the child slaves out of the mill and sweat-shop and give their unemployed fathers a chance to work. It will stop the butchering of the workers in time of peace as well as in time of war.

If you imagine "Making Work for the Unemployed" is unfair, just remember Ludlow and Calumet and don't forget Sacramento where the men who were unable to get work had their brains beaten out by the Hessians of the law and were knocked down and drenched to the skin with streams of ice-cold water manipulated by the city fire department, where the unemployed were driven out of the city and in the rain only to meet the pitchforks of the farmers. And what for? For the horrible crime of asking the governor of California—for A JOB!

This is the way the capitalist class uses the working class when they can no longer exploit them—in the name of Law and Order. Remember this when you MAKE WORK FOR THE UNEMPLOYED!

Published in the *International Socialist Review*, December 1914. —AB

SALT LAKE COUNTY JAIL
DECEMBER 2, 1914

SAM MURRAY

Dear Friend and Fellow Worker:

Received your letter and should have answered before, but have been busy working on some musical composition and whenever I get an "inspiration" I can't quit until it's finished.

I am glad to hear that you manage to make both ends meet, in spite of the industrial deal, but there is no use being pessimistic in this glorious land of plenty. Self preservation is, or should be, the first law of nature. The animals, when in a natural state, are showing us the way. When they are hungry they will always try to get something to eat or else they will die in the attempt. That's natural; to starve to death is unnatural.

No, I have not heard that song about "Tipperary" but if you send it as you said you would I might try to dope something out about that Frisco Fair. I am not familiar with the actual conditions of Frisco at present; and when I make a song I always try to picture things as they really are. Of course a little pepper and salt is allowed in order to bring out the facts more clearly.

If you send me that sheet music and give me some of the peculiarities and ridiculous points about the conditions in general on or about the fair ground, I'll try to do the best I can.

Yours for the OBU,
Joe Hill

Sam Murray wrote Hill asking him to write a song protesting unemployment and soup lines in the midst of the glamor of the San Francisco Fair. In response to Hill's request, Murray sent him "It's a Long, Long Way to Tipperary," then very popular with the soldiers of the British Army, and Joe Hill, parodying the song, wrote "It's a Long Way Down the Soupline." Soon afterwards, the Soupline song was sung up and down the West Coast.

SALT LAKE CITY
DECEMBER 7, 1914

KATIE PHAR
SPOKANE, WASHINGTON

Dear Friend and F.W.

I received your welcome letter and also your card with a nice fat turkey on it. Don't think for a moment that I have forgotten you but you see I have been quite busy composing some songs & music lately and that's the reason why I did not answer your letter sooner and I hope you will forgive me this time if I ask you real nice.

I am glad to hear that you are taking music lessons and intend to be a musician. You can always enjoy yourself when you know how to play music and you never need to be lonesome. I wish I had a chance to take music lessons when I was a kid, but I was not fortunate enough for that because I had to go to work at the age of 10, when my father died, and I had no money to spare for music lessons, but by trying hard I picked up what little I know about music without lessons. You see I've got music in the blood and it just comes natural to me to play any kind of an instrument.

I suppose you have lots of snowballs up around Spokane now. You tell me the snow hurts your eyes and if that's the case I would advise you to get a pair of blue glasses. It doesn't look very good for a young girl to wear glasses of course, but better that than spoiling your eyesight. Lots of people go blind from the snow.

> *Well with a kind greeting to you and all your friends I remain*
> *Yours for the O.B.U.,*
> *Joe Hill*

Joe Hill's references to having music in his blood is to the fact that his father, a railroad worker, was an amateur organist.

Facing page: A postcard sent to Charles Rudberg on December 18, 1914. Hill and Rudberg knew each other from their childhood in Gävle, Sweden. According to Rudberg's daughter, Frances Horn, the two met up again as adults in San Francisco in 1906. Rudberg had jumped ship the day before in San Francisco harbor and swum ashore, losing his shoes in the swim. As he was trudging up Market Street, barefooted, he ran into Joe Hill, who was surprised to see him. "What in the world

are you doing in America without shoes?" Hill asked. He then took Rudberg to the Sailors' Union and got him a pair of shoes and a job. The two traveled the West Coast together to Portland and back to San Pedro, where both were active in the Longshoremen's Union. Hill also sent postcards to Rudberg before he was incarcerated, all in the care of the Sailors' Union hall. —AB

SALT LAKE COUNTY JAIL
JANUARY 3, 1915

Dear Gus:

Jud Ricket was telling me the other day he had two or three contributions from you for the defense fund. You know I never was very sold on the sky pilots, but you're one preacher I'll let into heaven whenever I happen to be tending door. Ricket tells me funds keep coming in and there is going to be enough to finance the appeal clear to the supreme court. I'm still pretty sure no man is worth that much, but if I get sore and tell them to give the money to strike relief somewhere they don't pay any attention, so I have learned to keep still. Keep still and sit still. I'd make a first class toadstool.

I was thinking the other day, when the new year rolled around, that I've been in this calaboose almost a full year, and that's a long time to live on the kind of stew they serve here. The coffee is a little better than you used to make, but not enough to get excited about. Well, when we used to sit in the kitchen and drink that turpentine we never thought that pretty soon you'd be hoeing corn and I'd be where I am. I keep myself in good spirits by reminding myself that the worst is yet to come.

No chance to read anything here. Once a month or so a missionary of some kind comes around with a basket of books, but they're all full of moral uplift and angel food, and I'd rather read old letters over again than waste time on that. The missionary is a lot like you used to be. I think he prays for me.

Write me when you can. One thing this jail has made out of me is a good correspondent.

Your friend,

Joe

The May 23, 1914, issue of *Solidarity* carried the announcement that a Joe Hill Defense Committee had been elected by the Salt Lake locals of the IWW, and "every fellow worker who has sung any of Hill's songs ought to contribute, if it is only a dime."

SALT LAKE COUNTY JAIL
JANUARY 18, 1915
ELIZABETH GURLEY FLYNN
NEW YORK CITY, NEW YORK

Friend and F.W.

Saw your address in the "Sol" and am enclosing a letter for Jos. J Ettor and if you would try to locate him for me I would appreciate it very much. It is a receipt for some money and that's why I am anxious to locate him. While I am at it I want to thank you for what you have done for me and for the interest you have taken in my welfare, but on the square I'll tell you that all the notoriety stuff is making me dizzy in the head and I am afraid of getting more glory than I really am entitled to. I put most of the later years among the wharf-rats on the Pacific coast and am not there with the lime light stuff at all. I am feeling well under the circumstances and the boys and girls here are taking care of me like a mother would her first born babe—

With Best Regards to all
I am yours for the O.B.U.
Joe Hill

Joseph J. Ettor was a leading organizer for the IWW.

Joe Hill and Elizabeth Gurley Flynn had not met prior to this. With this letter there began a stream of correspondence which lasted until Joe Hill's execution. "Sol" is the IWW newspaper *Solidarity*.

SALT LAKE COUNTY JAIL
JANUARY 27, 1915
ELIZABETH GURLEY FLYNN
NEW YORK CITY, NEW YORK

Friend & F.W.

Your optimistic letter rec. o.k. and it certainly was very refreshing to receive a cheerful note. God knows that there are enough of gloomy hard-luck reports coming in about conditions in general. The "Workers Moratorium" or Pay-ye-by & by movement is certainly a very bright idea. If it works all right in England I see no reason why it shouldn't be a success in the US of A. How would it be to have a "certificate" of Moratorium to distribute among the un-

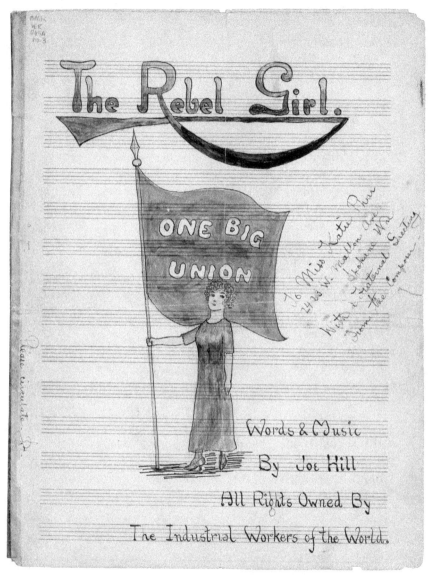

Although Hill discussed his work on "Rebel Girl" in letters to Sam Murray and Katie Phar, he kept it a secret from its likely inspiration, Elizabeth Gurley Flynn. Hill must have refined the song

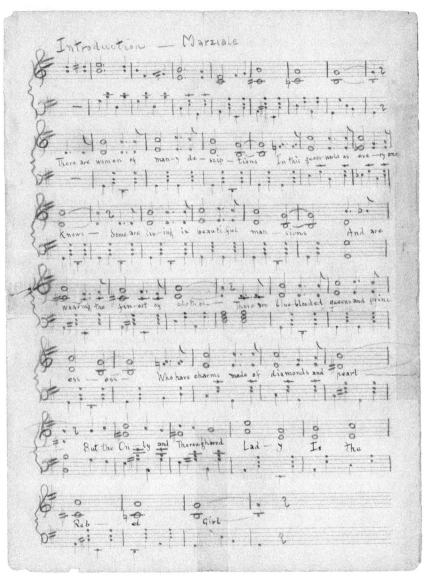

for months, first mentioning it in February 1914 and then sending the finished music to Phar in May 1915, having sent it to IWW headquarters in Chicago beforehand. —AB

employed which they, in turn, would hand to their respective Landlords when they come around for the rent? It may look like a worthless joke, of course, at first, but still if you think it over it has some value. It would show that the No-Rent League was an organized movement and not a temporary notion of an individual. It would also, through its originality, attract the attention of the public and of the news-hungry Press.

A Committee should also be appointed to visit the mayor and Judge Gary and tell them that the "Rent Problem" was solved and all the mayor would have to do would be to "recognize" the Certificate of Moratorium and refuse to let the "Law" evict any person holding such a certificate. That would take a load of worry off their chests and they wouldn't need to lose any more sleep about the "Rent Problem." If this plan works out all right then the next move would be to tackle the Food Problem and issue certificates "good for one meal" at any swell cafe in town and another one good for one "Dolling Up" at the Starvation Army 2nd Hand Store.

The thing the matter with the "Underdog" today is that he has drifted too far away from nature. The instinct that forces the animals of the jungle to make a bee line for the eats when hungry, has been chloroformed almost to death in the underdog by civilization and any old thing that has a tendency to arouse the instinct would be beneficial to the revolutionary movement. If suicide, or attempt to suicide, is a crime according to capitalistic laws, then the slow suicide by the starvation route most certainly must be a crime of the gravest kind.

Attached to the letter is a small sheet of paper, approximately the size of a playing card. On one side was:

DECLARATION OF MORATORIUM

Our Motto: "No Wages -- No Rent."

This is to certify that the holder of this certificate is a worker unable to find employment and is therefore entitled to shelter without the paying of rent until able to secure a position.

(signed) THE WORKERS MORATORIUM LEAGUE OF NEW YORK

On the other side there is an explanatory note by Joe Hill reading as follows:

P.S. My idea is to have something in this line printed and give it a kind of "legal" appearance, that is, use the kind of "type" used in legal documents. Then hold a mass meeting for the unemployed and explain the idea to them. Put the scheme up to the "bunch" and see what they think about it anyway. We started the scheme to print a song on the back of a throw away card in S. Pedro and it made a hit. J.H.

After P.S. Realizing that you have lots of writing to do I do not expect any answer to this letter. Joe.

Dee-lighted to see in the Papers that young John D. and Guggenheimer are becoming strong union men.

Judge Elbert H. Gary, president of the United States Steel Corporation, was chairman of the Mayor's Committee on Unemployment in New York City.

Joe Hill's suggestion "to print a song on the back of a throw away card" was used by the IWW Unemployed Union of New York. The union issued a red card on one side of which were printed quotations from Cardinal Henry Edward Manning, Father Bernard Vaughn, Oscar Wilde, and Jesus justifying the right of a starving man to obtain food and shelter without having to beg for them, and on the other side a song, "It's A Long Way Down to the Breadline," which was Charles Ashleigh's adaptation of Joe Hill's song, "It's A Long Way Down to the Soupline."

SALT LAKE COUNTY JAIL
JANUARY 19, 1915
GURLEY FLYNN

Enclosed find a young Xmas tree, and I wish you a Merry X-mas, Better late than never, don't che know.

Joe Hill

A pressed fern was enclosed with the card.

SALT LAKE COUNTY JAIL
FEBRUARY 13, 1915

SAM MURRAY

Friend and Fellow Worker:

Should have answered your letter before, but have been busy working on a song named "The Rebel Girl" (Words and Music), which I hope will help line up the women workers in the OBU, and I hope you will excuse me.

I see you made a big thing out of that Tipperary song. In fact, a whole lot more than I ever expected, I don't suppose that it would sell very well outside of Frisco, though by the way I got a letter from Swasey in NY and he told me that "Casey Jones" made quite a hit in London and "Casey Jones," he was an Angelino you know, and I never expected that he would leave Los Angeles at all.

The other day we got ten bucks from a company of soldiers stationed on the Mexican line. How is that old top? Maybe they are remembering some of the cigars in glass bottles that they smoked at the expense of the "Tierra e Libertad" bunch.

Don't know much about my case. The Sup. Court will "sit on" it sometime in the sweet bye and bye and that's all I know about it.

Give my best to the bunch.

Joe Hill

Sam Murray informed Joe Hill that the Wobblies in San Francisco had raised nearly fifty dollars by selling the Soupline (Tipperary) song for five cents for the Joe Hill Defense.

Joe Hill's case was appealed to the Supreme Court of Utah. Postponed several times, the appeal came before the Supreme Court on May 28, 1915.

SALT LAKE COUNTY JAIL
FEBRUARY 16, 1915

KATIE PHAR

Dear Friend and Fellow Worker:

Received your cheerful letter and also your pretty little valentine and I certainly am very pleased to be remembered by a brave little girl like you.

I see you are entertaining the Rebels of Spokane with your singing. That's right Katie, as long as we can keep on singing and keep the spirit up we are bound to win.

I made a new song named "The Rebel Girl" (Words and Music) and I am circulating it as fast as I can. Composing music without a piano is pretty hard you know and it will take some time to do it.

I got a lot of valentines this week, one nice one from Hilda and some from other places. Last Sunday there was about 30 boys and girls here to see me and I believe I have more friends now than I ever had in my life.

It is ten o'clock now and I am getting sleepy. Give my best to your father and all the rest.

As ever yours,
Joe Hill

25

SALT LAKE COUNTY JAIL
FEBRUARY 19, 1915
ELIZABETH GURLEY FLYNN
NEW YORK CITY, NEW YORK

Friend & F.W.

Rec. your welcome letter & am glad to note that there is something doing all the time in "little old N.Y." Yes I realize fully well now how hard it is to get the unemployed to do something for themselves. They are just like the chattel slaves of the South—when John Brown started out to Emancipate them, he found to his surprise that the slaves themselves were the ones who fought him the hardest. But still there are a few who have the nerve & audacity to think that "The World owes them a living" and we are acting accordingly and that is the encouraging feature about it. So the Soupline song made its way clean across the continent and little "Buster" is joining the chorus with the rest, eh? Well I hope that when he has grown up to be a big man that there will be no such thing as a soupline and that wage slaves will be a thing of the past. If F.W. Ashleigh wants to change the "Soupline song" to make it fit the brand of soup that they are dishing out in N.Y. he can hop right to it.

Well its 10 P.M. and I'll have to count the straws in my mattress. Can't afford to lose any of them nohow.

Yours for the O.B.U.
Joe Hill

Best Regard to all.

Have instructed Sec'y here to send data for the protest meeting and think he will try to do his best.

I would like to know how the Rent strike comes out in N.Y. Somebody around the hall having more time than you might drop me a line later on & let me know.

Elizabeth Gurley Flynn's six-year-old boy, Fred, was nicknamed Buster.
AB: Hill's remark about John Brown makes one wonder what he knew about the Harpers Ferry raid, since his brief reference is so plainly incorrect. John Brown, like Joe Hill, has a lot of mythology mixed in with his story. Clearly Hill was vexed by workers who did not take action for their own emancipation, and had an expectation that workers would be eager to take even substantial risks to achieve their own freedom. His general identification with Brown suggests that he had some exposure to, but not the precise details of, the history of antislavery movements.

SALT LAKE COUNTY JAIL
MARCH 4, 1915

MISS KATIE PHAR
SPOKANE, WASHINGTON

Dear Friend & F.W.

Your welcome letter received O.K. and am glad to note that things are booming in "Spoke" from a rebel's point of view. I have been pretty busy lately but I will send you some of my compositions as soon as I can get around to it. So you are going to learn to play the violin, eh? That always was my favorite instrument. I would rather play the fiddle than eat. I bet you will like it too.

With best regards to your folks, I am as Ever
Your Friend
Joe Hill

SALT LAKE COUNTY JAIL
MARCH 10, 1915

ELIZABETH G. FLYNN
NEW YORK CITY, NEW YORK

Friend & F.W.

Received both of your very interesting letters and I thought they were too good to have them laying around in my "apartment" so I mailed them to Ed Rowan & Co. Have been trying to figure out how you can have all the time to write me such nice, fat letters and hold big meetings every night besides, but I guess you are like Tommy Edison, you don't sleep more than four hours a day & work twenty.

Your Pat Quinlan got a pretty rough deal. Even the capitalist papers have to admit it. I see I have often been trying to figure out some way to counteract the high handed tactics used by the dispensers of "Justice." It is easy enough to see a remedy from an individual point of view but when one looks at it as a class problem, then it becomes quite complex. It is plain enough tho that the idea of fighting organized capital with money is not the correct way.

I hope you & the other F.W.'s will not get into trouble again. I think you've had your share of it already but then as you say, there's nothing else to be expected for the vanguards of the Revolutionary movement. F.W. Tom Murphy got released the 9th of March after serving one year for the "rioting" here at a street meeting. Guess you know the particulars of it all, all ready.

I think the organization should use all its resources to keep the "live wires" on the outside. I mean organizers and orators. When they are locked up they are dead as far as the organization [is] concern[ed]. A fellow like myself, for instance, can do just as well in jail. I can dope out my music & "poems" in here and slip them out through the bars and the world will never know the difference. I have plenty of magazines and things to read. I am subscribing to the Denver Post also. Would like to have our papers & pamphlets of course, but.

Well say Hello to Erickson and all the rest of "the bunch" in little old N.Y.

Yours for the O.B.U.

Joe Hill

Ed Rowan, Secretary of the IWW local in Salt Lake City, headed the Joe Hill Defense Committee.

Patrick Quinlan, IWW organizer, had been sentenced from two to seven years at hard labor in the state prison at Trenton, New Jersey, for his role in the Paterson silk strike of 1913. His sentence was part of a brutal oppression of the fundamental rights of the strikers by the Paterson authorities.

SALT LAKE COUNTY JAIL
NO DATE

(excerpt)

Headed "From another letter to Vanderleith"

No, Van, I don't dislike the poems of ___ and ___ and the others. I know they mean well, and the poems are swell, but it kind of gets my goat to be mushed up that way. You know I always intended to go it alone, but somebody on the coast started the ball rolling, and here I am a martyr, a Tin-Jesus. Well honestly, wouldn't that jar ye? . . .

The Supreme Court will "sit on" my case May 2d. Judge Hilton came here from Denver just in time to save it from being postponed again and believe me I am grateful to the "Grand Old Man" for doing it. He is certainly there with the goods. He is confident of getting a reversal, he says. . . .

I realize as you do that the women are doing wonderful work for our organization and I think it would be a good idea to spend a little more money and energy in organizing the women workers especially in the big industrial centers in the East. There is too much energy going to waste organizing locals in "jerk water towns" of no industrial importance. A town like San Diego for instance where the main "industry" consists of "catching suckers" is not worth a whoop in Hell from a rebel's point of view. Still there has been more money spent on that place than there ever was on Pittsburgh, Detroit and other manufacturing towns of great importance. Organization is just like dripping water on a blotter—if you drip enough of it in the center it will soak through clean to the edges.

The Vanderleith letters were transcribed and attached to a letter sent by A. C. Pollok, Theodore Pollok, and Charlotte Anita Whitney to Frank Walsh, chair of the Commission on Industrial Relations, established by Congress in 1912. Walsh was a politically connected Missouri lawyer closely linked to progressive reformers. Their letter to Walsh does not survive; his response, dated August 20, 1915, states:

> This is the first definite information which I have received in regard to the general outline of Hill's case. I think I gather his attitude, as well as an understanding of the forces which seem about to take his life from what you have written me. . . . I am absolutely at a loss to know what I can do for Hill at this distance. I recoil with the utmost horror at the thought of this whole business of the killing of human beings in the name of law.
>
> What you have written me about Hill's case, of course, strikes a very deep chord of sympathy in my heart and I would do anything in my power to assist him. I know Judge Hilton as a man of vast ability and resource, so that I must conclude that all available legal steps will be taken.
>
> You are right in excluding all hope of action by the United States Supreme Court. It never takes jurisdiction of criminal cases which have been passed upon by the courts of the respective states. In fact, through the interpretations of the various sections of the Constitution by that court, the right to a writ of error from it has become a mere paper one.
>
> I will accept any reasonable suggestion that you may make as to what I could do to help Hill out.

Walsh also received an appeal from Tom Mooney of the International Workers' Defense League on October 11, 1915, and a copy of O. N. Hilton's October 17, 1915, open letter to the Utah Board of Pardons. There is no record of Walsh taking any public action on Hill's behalf.

The names of the poets mentioned in the letter were removed by whomever transcribed it for Pollok, possibly Vanderleith himself. One name is likely to be Ralph Chaplin, who was serving as the editor of the IWW newspaper *Solidarity* and published a florid ode he wrote to Hill. —AB

SALT LAKE COUNTY JAIL
MARCH 22, 1915

SAM MURRAY
NAPA, CALIFORNIA

Friend and Fellow Worker:

Yours of March 13th at hand. I note that you have gone "back to nature" again and I must confess that it is making me a little homesick when you mention that "little cabin in the hills" stuff. You can talk about your dances, picnics and blow outs, and it won't affect me, but the "little cabin" stuff always gets my goat. That's the only life I know.

Yes, that Tipperary song is spreading like the smallpox they say. Sec. 69 tells me that there is a steady stream of silver from 'Frisco on account of it. The unemployed all over the country have adopted it as a marching song in their parades, and in New York City they changed it to some extent, so as to fit the brand of soup dished out in N.Y. They are doing great work in N.Y. this year. The unemployed have been organized and have big meetings every night. Gurley Flynn, Geo. Swasey (the human phonograph) and other live ones are there, and Gurley F. tells me things are looking favorable for the OBU. The hearing of my case has been postponed they say, and they are trying to make me believe that is for my benefit, but I'll tell you it is damn hard for me to see where the benefit comes in at; damn hard.

> *Well, I have about a dozen letters to answer,*
> *Yours as ever,*
> *Joe Hill.*

Section 69 was the IWW branch in Utah. —AB

SALT LAKE COUNTY JAIL
MAY 7, 1915

KATIE PHAR
SPOKANE, WASHINGTON

Dear Friend and Fellow Worker,

Yours received and am glad to note you are getting along fine with your music lessons. Am sending you through the local Secretary two of my songs and would like to hear how you like them. One of the songs, "The Rebel Girl," was sung at several big meetings in Chicago and was making a big hit they are telling me.

I had the pleasure to shake hands with Gurley Flynn yesterday and she told me that she would be glad to see you when she comes to Spokane. If you would practice up on one of the songs you could help her a whole lot by singing it at her meeting in Spokane. "The Rebel Girl" would be best I think because Gurley Flynn is certainly some Rebel Girl and when you and her get together there will be "two of a kind." Ha, Ha.

Well, I hope you will help me to introduce the songs around Spokane, and lend them out to people who want to learn them because I am only writing two copies for each large city. I would like to make two copies for every Rebel in U.S., but—it can't be done.

My case will come up this month some time and everything looks good.

As ever, Your Friend, Regards to All,
Joe Hill

I enclose a nice hair ribbon for you. *Joe*

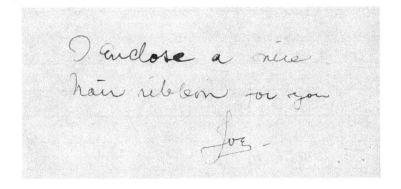

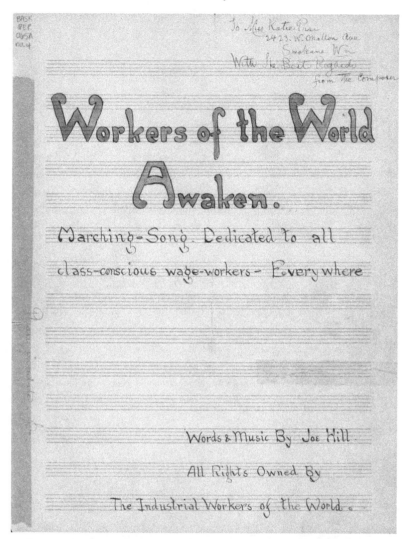

The second song Hill references in his May 7, 1915, letter to Katie Phar was undoubtedly "Workers of the World, Awaken." The lyrics clearly borrow from Eugène Pottier and Pierre De Geyter's "The Internationale," which the IWW included in its earliest songbooks. Remarkably, Hill created complex sheet music for "Awaken" without an instrument to reference, as he did with his other original jailhouse compositions, "Rebel Girl" and "Don't Take My Papa Away from Me." Later, the IWW published all of these songs as professional sheet music. —AB

SALT LAKE COUNTY JAIL
JUNE 6, 1915

SAM MURRAY

Friend and Fellow Worker:

Your welcome letter received, and am glad to note that you are still sticking to your "little cabin in the hills." I would like to get a little of that close to nature stuff myself for a couple of months in order to regain a little vitality, and a little flesh on my rotting bones. My case was argued on the 28th of May, and according to Judge Hilton, the results were satisfactory. He says he is sure of securing a reversal, and if so, there hardly will be another trial, for the simple reason that there won't be anything to try, if I can get a lawyer that will defend me.

With best wishes to all the rebels, Yours for the O.B.U.,
Joe Hill.

P.S. I've just found out that the Superior Court judges are getting ready to go on their vacation until next fall, so I guess there won't be anything decided on my case for some time. But "everything comes to him who waits" they say, and that's the only consolation I got now.

Joe.

Judge Orrin Nelson Hilton of Denver, the distinguished attorney for the Western Federation of Miners, was persuaded to come to Hill's legal defense late in his appeal by Mrs. Virginia Snow Stephen of Salt Lake City on behalf of the IWW Defense Committee. Judge Hilton arranged for Soren X. Christensen, a Salt Lake City lawyer to become his associate in the case, but he himself argued the appeal before the Utah Supreme Court.

AB: Stephen was the daughter of a former president of the Mormon Church, Lorenzo Snow, and a faculty member of the art department of the University of Utah. Police shot and killed unarmed Salt Lake Wobbly Roy J. Horton after an argument on October 30, 1915, and Stephen sang at his funeral. She was fired from the University of Utah several months later.

UTAH STATE PRISON
JULY 7, 1915

ELIZABETH GURLEY FLYNN
CHICAGO, ILLINOIS

Dear Friend & F.W.

Rec. Your letter at the Co. Jail. Was denied a new trial and was immediately moved to the State Prison where I am now. Will be taken down to the city pretty soon and re-sentenced. I have no comments to make regarding the decision. You know the details of the case pretty well and you may draw your own conclusions about it. I don't know if anything can be done to the case as I have not heard from Hilton yet. I was told though that the case could be taken to the U.S. Supreme Court just for the cost of having the transcripts made out which would not exceed $100.00, but I am not very posted on the subject myself & could not say for sure what it would cost. You see it would not be necessary to have a lawyer in Washington D.C. and that's why the expenses would not be so very heavy. Of course it would take two or three years before the case would be taken up because there are something like two thousand cases on the docket but if we could get justice that wouldn't make any difference. Even if I should die before the decision were handed down, I am only a drop in the bucket & this is a fight where individuals don't count. My right hand was shot all to splinters anyway when I was arrested and it doesn't matter much where I go to but to tell you the truth I hate to lay down as long as there is a fighting chance.

Yours for the O.B.U.

Joe Hill

Hill was denied a new trial by the Supreme Court of Utah on July 2, 1915. He was later resentenced to be shot on October 1, 1915. For Hill's account of how his right hand was shot, see his September 28 letter to the Board of Pardons.

UTAH STATE PRISON
JULY 14, 1915

Ed Rowan & FWs

What does the organization think proper action to take now? My life is a drop in the bucket, but there is a principle involved [in] back of this case! And to be honest, I don't want to lie down, as long as we have the least fighting chance. I don't know any thing about the future, but am prepared for anything.

As Ever,
Joe

Hill maintained from the moment he was arrested until he was executed that the principle he was upholding was that under the American system of justice a defendant need not prove he is innocent. It is the obligation of the prosecutor to prove the defendant guilty beyond a reasonable doubt. In short, it is the sacred right of every man accused of committing a crime to the presumption of innocence. "If my life will help some other working man to a fair trial," he announced on September 19, 1915, through his counsel, Soren X. Christensen, "I am ready to give it. If by giving my life I can aid others to the fairness denied me, I have not lived in vain."

UTAH STATE PRISON
JULY 14, 1915

O. N. HILTON
DENVER, COLORADO

Dear Judge:

Yours received O.K. Was removed to the state prison immediately after the decision was handed down, where I am now. I realize full well that there is only one problem to consider at present and that is the financial one. If I'd had the money to begin with I would not have had to depend on "charity attorneys" and consequently would not be where I am now.

I am not very well posted on matters concerning the U.S. Supreme Court, but I have been told that it would not be necessary to have an attorney in Washington, D.C., for the purpose of delivering an oral argument, and if that is a fact it seems to me the cost of the appeal would be reduced to some extent by cutting out R.R. fares, etc.

If the case cannot be appealed without having an attorney in Washington,

D.C., then I am afraid we'll have to let it go as it is—because I can not expect my friends to starve themselves in order to save my life.

I would of course like to have the case appealed, if the cost is not prohibitive; and if the case is appealed I would not have anybody but you preparing the appeal, because I've had my fill of "tin horn shysters." If you could give us the approximate cost of an appeal to the U.S. Supreme Court, and also tell us if you could handle the case yourself, from your Denver office, we would know better what to do. Wm. D. Haywood and Ed Rowan would of course be parties to inform about all financial matters concerning the case.

Of course I am not in a position to know if anything is being done or not, but from previous experience, I draw the conclusion that if you don't do anything for me, it won't be done.

But I also realize that you are not in the business for your health, and I also know that you, unlike many others in your profession, have only one way to get money, and that's from your clients; and if the client cannot produce it, you'll of course have to drop his case.

Well, Mr. Hilton, if circumstances are such that nothing can be done, I want to thank you for what you have already done for me. And you can just bet your bottom dollar that I show this gang of highbinders that are operating here in the name of Justice, how a MAN should die.

Respectfully yours,
—J. Hillstrom

Hilton wrote two letters in reply. The first, dated Denver, Colorado, July 19, 1915, read:

Dear Joe:

Yours of the 14th just at hand and I inclose you a letter, just received this A.M. from Haywood, also one from Rowan and a telegram rec'd yesterday from Christensen. I answered the latter yesterday by wire telling him that if he felt that a rehearing was of no use, not to make it but to apply to the Pardoning Board for a commutation of sentence. I am moved to this conclusion for a variety of reasons principally from the fact that a hearing before the Supreme Ct. at Washington would necessitate a trip there and this of course would be expensive and we are without funds. The irony of the whole miserable matter is intensified when we know that it could all have been avoided if you had even a decent defense in the court below. I shall co-operate in every way with Haywood and write him again fully to-day. If you conclude to have the case taken to the United States Supreme Ct. get word of it to Christensen in some way and have him file application for a rehearing for without it we can go no further. Frankly however I do not believe it will avail us anything. I am generally distressed as I read your letters, yet admire the manly, courageous stand you take—*for good game people are scarce.* I shall hope to hear from you from time to time.

> *Sincerely yr. friend*
> *O. N. Hilton.*
> *Excuse pencil*

The second letter, dated Denver, Colorado, July 20, 1915, read:

My dear Hillstrom

I thought about your case half the night and conclude to say a word more in addition to what I wrote yesterday. I am at a serious disadvantage being so far away and so cannot conclude safely just what is the best way to pursue if any. My present notion is to apply to the Pardoning Board for a commutation. Nothing else is left as we are utterly without funds to make any further battle and even this may be futile as the Board is composed of the members of the Supreme Court, the Atty Gen. and the Gov. of the state. These men have already passed on your case with the exception of the Gov. and he has been in receipt of threatening letters foolishly sent him by some members of the I.W.W.

It is very distressful for me to decide just what is wise to advise and I cannot so do until I hear from Haywood; but it does seem this is all there is left, altho the outlook is not promising. See if you cannot reach Christensen and get his ideas. He is through with that investigation and his judgment of local matters and conditions would be superior to mine. I will also write him to-day and ask him to interest himself at least to the extent of giving you his opinion. The letter that you wrote me touched me deeply and I want you to feel that what the boys owe me for my services already cuts no figure with me and I would gladly renounce it all and as much more if I could accomplish any good thing for you and right this monstrous injustice that has been done you. If I am unable to so to do, I know you will appreciate that it is not for the lack of money which you have not got, or a sincere belief in you as a man, and your innocence.

Sincerely your friend,
O. N. Hilton

William "Big Bill" Haywood was the IWW's General Secretary-Treasurer.

UTAH STATE PRISON
JULY 15, 1915

GURLEY FLYNN
CHICAGO, ILLINOIS

Dear Friend & F.W.

Yours of July 8th at hand and I am always glad to get a line from you. Hope you will be able to get your well-deserved vacation, as you told me you had planned, and take your little boy out "to see a cow"—to use your own words. Yes Gurley, the motion for a new trial was denied and although I must admit that it jolted me a little when I first heard it, I am taking it more philosophically now. All you've got to do is to look around you a little—you can plainly see that there is a movement on foot to systematically drain the resources of Organized Labor all over the country. Look at the Ford & Suhr case in Calif. The Lawson case in Colorado, etc. You've got to hand it to "Kaiser Bill." He knew what he was talking about when he said that laws and treaties are nothing but "scraps of paper." He said a whole mouth full that time old Bill did. I see in the papers that Harry Thaw was declared "sane" and will be free pretty soon. Isn't that nice? If I could afford to have one of them "brain storms" maybe they'd let me go too, but them brainstorms are luxuries that us wobblies have to do without.

I don't know what the future got in store for me but I do know that I am ready to meet anything no matter what it is. There has been some talk about taking the case to the U.S. Sup. Court but I don't know what to think about it. There has been enough of money expended on my case already. I certainly approve of publicity and "other methods" that you mentioned in your letter, however I asked Hilton to make a little write up just for that purpose copy of which you can have by asking Big Bill. Well Gurley dear, I'm proud to have a Rebel Girl like you for a friend and in case you should not see me again I wish you all the luck in the world and hoping that you will live to see the day when

Labor's Cause, for which you fought so splendidly, shall triumph, I remain,

Fraternally Yours,

Joe Hill

Richard Ford and Herman D. Suhr, two IWW organizers, were sentenced to life imprisonment as a result of an incident arising out of the Hop Workers' strike at Wheatland, California, August 3, 1914. A decade-long campaign eventually freed them.

John R. Lawson, a United Mine Workers' leader, was convicted of murder and sentenced to life imprisonment as a result of incidents arising out of the Colorado coal strike of 1913–14, a highlight of which was the "Ludlow Massacre." He was freed on appeal by the Colorado Supreme Court in 1917.

On June 25, 1906, Harry K. Thaw, a thirty-five-year-old Pittsburgh millionaire, shot and killed Stanford White, the famous architect, at the Madison Square Garden Roof Garden. Thaw charged that White had once seduced his (Thaw's) wife, Evelyn Nesbit, and that he had killed him to avenge her. In 1908 in a second trial, after the first jury could not reach an agreement, Thaw was found not guilty by reason of insanity, and was consigned to Matteawan Hospital for the Criminally Insane.

UTAH STATE PRISON
JULY 22, 1915

WM. D. HAYWOOD
CHICAGO, ILLINOIS

Fellow Worker:

Am in receipt of a letter from Judge Hilton and after reading it I came to the conclusion that we cannot afford to carry the case to the U.S. Supreme Court and have decided to drop it. I instructed the local Sec. and Defense Comm. to not pay another cent to *anybody* and that will of course, close the case automatically. I am reading the daily papers here and I can see where the money can be used to great advantage at present by the Organization and there is no use to be sentimental about it Bill; we can not afford to let the whole organization go bankrupt just on account of one individual.

Well—old War-Hoss—I want to thank you for what you have done for me, and hoping that you will live to see the final "cave-in" when the rotten props of capitalism will go from under and the working class will rule the World, I remain

Yours for Industrial Freedom.

Joe Hill

UTAH STATE PRISON
JULY 22, 1915

Ed Rowan & FW's:

Have written to Hilton & Haywood and informed them of the fact that the case is dropped. I enclose another letter from Hilton. Wish you would send the two of them to E.G.F. in N.Y. I think she can use them for the purpose of publicity. Well I feel a lot better after dropping the case. It seems as if a ton of lead had been lifted from my chest and hoping that you feel the same, I remain

As Ever,

Joe

The two letters written by Hilton were the ones quoted above. Hill's decision to drop any further appeal was overruled. The IWW vowed to "fight this to the very end."

UTAH STATE PRISON
JULY 24, 1915
ELIZABETH GURLEY FLYNN
NEW YORK CITY, NEW YORK

Dear Friend & F.W.

Your welcome letter at hand and am glad to note that you are "homeward bound" where you will get a well deserved rest and get rid of your bad cold.

I wrote a letter to Judge Hilton a week ago and asked him to state the approximate cost of taking my case to the U.S. Sup. Court. In his reply he did not state the amount but he explained to me what an enormous amount of preliminary red tape there is to such a transaction, and realizing that red tape is something that has to be paid for by the foot, I immediately came to the conclusion, after reading Hilton's letter, that "It can't be done." After reaching that conclusion, I got busy with my lead pencil & notified all parties handling my Defense to drop the case right there & then and give their attention to something worth while. We cannot afford to weaken the resources of the whole organization and weaken its fighting strength just on account of one individual. Common sense will tell you that Gurley.

There will be plenty new rebels come in to "fill the gaps," as the "war-news" puts it, one more or less does not count any more than it does in the European War. Well Gurley give my Best to the advance guard in NY City and last but not least to Little Buster.

Yours As Ever,
Joe

Elizabeth Gurley Flynn had just completed a cross-country speaking tour during which she had visited Hill in the County Jail in Salt Lake City.

UTAH STATE PRISON
AUGUST 6, 1915

ELIZABETH GURLEY FLYNN
NEW YORK CITY, NEW YORK

Dear Friend and F.W.

Yours of July 25th at hand and I note that you are taking a very optimistic view of the financial situation. Very well Gurley—I have absolutely no desire to be one of them what-ye-call-em-martyrs and if there is any way of carrying the case to the U.S. Sup. Court, it is of course O.K. with me. I'll tell you honestly though, that you made me feel ashamed of myself when you donated the $5 that somebody gave you for "a treat" and although I know that you gave it with the best of spirit I almost believe that you were robbing yourself by doing so.

Well I guess I must admit that I am absolutely helpless and unable to do anything for myself.

I was taken up to the court the other day and resentenced to be shot on the 1st day of Oct. this year. I am getting along fairly well here—being the air is purer & not so hot as it is down in the Co. jail. Well I don't know anything new, and will close for this time. Take good care of your throat and, what ever you do—don't try to overthrow the "System" all alone.

With best wishes I am
Fraternally yours
Joe Hill

UTAH STATE PRISON
AUGUST 12, 1915

SAM MURRAY

Friend and Fellow Worker:

Yours of August 5th at hand and as you see I have been moved to the State prison. The appeal was denied and I was up in court the other day and sentenced to be shot on the first day of October. We were all very much surprised at the decision, because we thought that I would be granted a new trial anyway. But as Judge Hilton says "the records of the lower court are so rotten they had to be covered somehow." I guess you can draw your conclusions from that statement. I wanted to drop the case right there and then, but from reports received from all parts of the country, I think that the case will be carried to the U.S. Supreme Court. I didn't think I'd be worth any more money. You know human life is kind of cheap this year anyway—but I guess the organization thinks otherwise and majority rule goes with me.

Well, I don't know anything new and hoping that you are successful in snaring the elusive doughnut, I remain, Yours for the O.B.U.

Joe Hill

It was finally decided not to carry the case to the U.S. Supreme Court because it would probably rule there was no federal question involved. The Joe Hill case was then carried to the Utah Board of Pardons, which announced a special session on September 18 to consider the appeal.

UTAH STATE PRISON
AUGUST 15, 1915

EDITOR, SALT LAKE TELEGRAM
SALT LAKE CITY, UTAH

Sir—

I have noticed that there have been some articles in your paper wherein the reason why I discharged my attorneys E.B. Scott and E.D. McDougall, was discussed pro and con. If you will kindly allow me a little space I think I might be able to throw a little light on the question.

There were several reasons why I discharged or tried to discharge these attorneys. The main reason, however, was because they never attempted to cross examine the witnesses for the state, and failed utterly to deliver the points of the defense.

When I asked them why they did not use the records of the preliminary hearing and pin the witnesses down to their former statements, they blandly informed me that the preliminary hearing had nothing to do with the district court hearing and that under the law they had no right to use said records.

I picked up a record myself and tried to look at it, but Mr. Scott took it away from me, stating that "it would have a bad effect on the jury." I then came to the conclusion that Scott and McDougall were not there for the purpose of defending me, and I did just what any other men would have done—I stood up and showed them the door. But, to my great surprise, I discovered that the presiding Judge had the power to compel me to have these attorneys, in spite of all my protests.

The main and only fact worth considering however, is this: I never killed Morrison and do not know a thing about it.

He was, as the records plainly show, killed by some enemy for the sake of revenge, and I have not been in this city long enough to make an enemy. Shortly before my arrest, I came down from Park City, where I was working in the mines. Owing to the prominence of Mr. Morrison, there had to be a "goat," and the undersigned being, as they thought, a friendless tramp, a Swede, and worst of all, an I.W.W., had no right to live anyway, and was therefore selected to be "the goat."

There were men sitting on my jury, the foreman being one of them, who were never subpoenaed for the case. There are errors and perjury that are screaming to high heaven for mercy, and I know that I, according to the laws of the land, am entitled to a new trial, and the fact that the supreme court does not grant it to me only proves that the beautiful term, "equality before the law," is merely an empty phrase in Salt Lake City.

Here is what Judge Hilton of Denver, one of the greatest authorities on law, has to say about it:

"The decision of the supreme court surprised me greatly, but the reason the verdict was affirmed is, I think, on account of the rotten records made by the lower court."

This statement shows plainly why the motion for a new trial was denied and there is no explanation necessary. In conclusion I wish to state that my records are not quite as black as they have been painted.

In spite of all the hideous pictures and all the bad things said and printed about me, I had only been arrested once before in my life, and that was in San Pedro, Cal. At that time of the stevedores' and dock workers' strike I was secretary of the strike committee, and I suppose I was a little too active to suit the chief of the burg, so he arrested me and gave me thirty days in the city jail for "vagrancy"—and there you have the full extent of my "criminal record."

I have worked hard for a living and paid for everything I got, and my spare time I spend by painting pictures, writing songs and composing music.

Now, if the people of the State of Utah want to shoot me without giving me half a chance to state my side of the case, then bring on your firing squads—I am ready for you.

I have lived like an artist and I shall die like an artist. Respectfully yours,
Joseph Hillstrom

The *Salt Lake Telegram*, which published Hill's letter on August 22, 1915, introduced it as follows:

From the death house of the state prison Joseph Hillstrom has written a letter to the editor of the *Telegram* laying his case before the people. It is the message of a man who is doomed and for whom there seems little hope. The date of his execution is little more than a month away.

Hillstrom closes his statement with this declaration: "I have lived like an artist and I shall die like an artist."

About halfway through the state's presentation of its case, Hill created a "sensation" by stopping the proceedings and demanding that his attorneys be discharged. "I have three prosecuting attorneys here," he said (meaning the prosecuting attorneys plus the two defense attorneys), "and I intend to get rid of two of them. Mr. Scott and Mr. McDougall, do you see that door? Get out of that door, I am through with you." After discharging his attorneys, Hill announced that he would handle his own case, that he wanted to recall the state's witnesses and cross-examine them himself. "I will prove that I was not at the Morrison grocery store that night. You can bring buckets of blood if you like, but you can't fool me." The bailiff forced Hill to take his seat, and his discharged counsel was directed to proceed with his cross-examination of a state witness. When Hill interrupted and ordered Scott out of the room, the attorney replied that he was present "by order of the court." "But can't I discharge my own attorneys?" Hill demanded. "You can," replied Judge Ritchie, "but I have asked the attorneys to stay here for a while as friends of the court, and they will cross-examine the witnesses just as before. You may take part in the proceedings. The trial moved ahead with Hill continuing to be represented by two attorneys (in whom he had lost confidence) plus his own efforts. Christensen joined the defense later in the trial. A large part of the argument among Hill, his attorneys, and the judge was conducted in the presence of the jury. The jury, it is clear, should immediately have been excused.

Hill's reference to "all the hideous pictures and all the bad things said and printed about me" applies to the campaign in the Salt Lake City press shortly after he was arrested to portray him as a "hardened criminal." The *Deseret Evening News* of January 24, 1914, under the headline, "Hillstrom's Crime Record of California Sent Here," told a story, furnished by the police, that Hill had been arrested in Los Angeles in June 1913, and "accused of participation in street car holdups." On January 24, 1914, the *Deseret Evening News* printed what was said to be a "Bertillon photograph" (a mugshot) supplied by the Los Angeles police and said to show Hill after he was arrested as a car robbery suspect. The picture was denounced by Hill's friends as "false" and the paper never reprinted it.

"Motive Probably Revenge," the *Deseret Evening News* announced on January 12, 1914, two days after the murder of Morrison and his son and several days before Hill was arrested. "The generally accepted theory," it continued, "is that the highwaymen who were routed by J. G. Morrison on two occasions within the past 10 years when they were fired upon by Morrison and forced into street battles with the fearless grocer and the police, returned to the Morrison store and killed the proprietor through revenge."

UTAH STATE PRISON
AUGUST 18, 1915

ELIZABETH GURLEY FLYNN
NEW YORK CITY, NEW YORK

Friend and F. W.

Yours of Aug 3 at hand and should have answered before but there is nothing of importance happening and I have nothing new to tell you.

I was resentenced to be shot on the first day of Oct. and according to the local press the only hope for me is the Board of Pardons. That means, I suppose, that they are going to give me life if I beg for it real nice. I'll tell you Gurley, I never did like the ring of the word "pardon" and I'd rather be buried dead, than buried alive. I never "licked the hand that holds the whip" yet and I don't see why I should have to start it now.

Well give my best to the bunch.

Yours Joe Hill

I enclose two clippings from the local press. Joe

UTAH STATE PRISON
SEPTEMBER 7, 1915

ELIZABETH GURLEY FLYNN
NEW YORK CITY, NEW YORK

Dear Friend and F.W.

Rec. your letter some time ago but not having anything of importance to tell you did not answer right away. I am receiving quite a few letters from all parts of the country. Some from Christian societies and others less Christian, Wobblies, and it all helps to pass the time away. Bill tells me that he is going to "run" "The Rebel Girl" and put her on the market. Hope she'll show some speed—on the West Coast the other song "Workers of the World, Awaken" is making quite a hit, they are telling me. They say "the Rebel Girl" is "a little hard to make out" and I guess it is a little more complex than the other one. The easterners have more "Kultur" than the western roughnecks and I guess that might have something to do with it too. Yes I should swan, it would be kind of amusing to see you boil spuds, iron clothes, and sling the ink all at the same time.

I have heard that there is a branch of rebels that call themselves "impossibilists" but I'd bet a gold mine against a doughnut that you are not affiliated with that bunch at all. It doesn't seem to be anything impossible for you.

Well I don't know a thing about the case. My attorneys told me to leave everything to them and that makes it pretty soft for me, having somebody else to do the worrying for me. Pretty soft indeed. With Best Wishes to Everybody round the Spud-pot and also to the bunch around the Hall I remain

Yours for the O.B.U.
Joe Hill

Did you receive the Printed "Brief" Argument of my case? It was sent to you from S.L. City.

The "impossibilists" were those in the IWW who believed that the struggle for immediate demands was a waste of time and that the only activity that counted was the circulation of propaganda for the immediate inauguration of Socialism.

The "Brief" was *Appellant's Brief in the State of Utah, Plaintiff and Respondent vs. Joseph Hillstrom in the Supreme Court of the State of Utah*. There is a copy in File 2573, "Joseph Hillstrom," Woodrow Wilson Papers, Library of Congress.

UTAH STATE PRISON
SEPTEMBER 9, 1915

SAM MURRAY
SAN FRANCISCO, CALIFORNIA

Friend and Fellow Worker:

Yours received O.K. Glad to hear that things are picking up. I see that you are employed at making bait for the German "sharks." Well war certainly shows up the capitalist system in the right light. Millions of men are employed at making ships and others are hired to sink them. Scientific management, eh, wot?

As far as I can see, it doesn't make much difference which side wins, but I hope that *one side will win*, because a draw would only mean another war in a year or two. All these silly priests and old maid sewing circles that are moaning about peace at this time should be locked up in the crazy house as a menace to society. The war is the finest training school for rebels in the world and for anti-militarists as well, and I hope that all the S.S. bills in the country will go over there.

Well, Sam, I don't know anything about my case. My attorneys told me to leave it all to them, and that makes it pretty soft for me to have someone else do the worrying for me. I believe your good work on the coast is being felt at this end of the line, though.

With best wishes I am as ever yours,
Joe Hill.

Hill's attitude towards the war was a pretty fair reflection of the general IWW view that it was inevitable that the United States, as an imperialist nation, would be drawn into the imperialist war in Europe, and that the workers should not waste their energy trying to prevent it but begin to prepare for the greater class struggle certain to emerge after the war.

UTAH STATE PRISON
SEPTEMBER 28, 1915

TO THE UTAH BOARD OF PARDONS

A Few Reasons Why I Demand A New Trial

When I was up before the highest authorities of the state of Utah I stated that I wanted a new trial and nothing but a new trial, and I will now try to state some reasons why I am entitled to that privilege. Being aware of the fact that my past record has nothing to do with the facts of this case, I will not dwell upon that subject beyond saying that I have worked all my life as a mechanic and at times as a musician. The mere fact that the prosecution never attempted to assail my reputation proves that it is clean. I will therefore commence at the time of my arrest.

On the night of January 14, 1914, I was lying in a bed at the Eselius house in Murray, a town located seven miles from Salt Lake City, suffering from a bullet wound in the chest. Where or why I got that wound is nobody's business but my own. I know that I was not shot in the Morrison store and all the so-called evidence that is supposed to show I was is fabrications pure and simple. As I was lying there half asleep, I was aroused by a knock on the door, somebody opened the door and in came four men with revolvers in their hands. A shot rang out and a bullet passed right over my chest, grazing my shoulder and penetrating my right hand through the knuckles, crippling me for life. There was absolutely no need of shooting me at that time because I was helpless as a baby and had no weapons of any kind. The only thing that saved my life at that time was the officer's inefficiency with fire-arms.

I was then brought up to the county jail where I was given a bunk and went to sleep immediately. The next morning I was pretty sore on account of being shot in three places. I asked to be taken to a hospital but was instead taken upstairs to a solitary cell, and told that I was charged with murder and had better confess right away. I did not know anything about any murder and told them so. They still insisted on that I confess, and told me they would take me to a hospital and "treat me right" if I did. I told them I knew nothing of any murder. They called me a "liar," and after that I refused to answer all questions. I grew weaker and weaker, and for three or four days I was hovering between life and death, and I remember an officer coming up and telling me that according to the doctor's statement I had only one hour to live. I could, of course name all these officers if I wanted to, but I want it distinctly understood that I am not trying to knock any officers, because I realize that they were only doing their duty, and in my opinion the officers who were in charge of the county jail then, were as good officers as can be found anywhere. Well! I finally pulled through because I made up my mind not to die.

When the time came for my preliminary hearing, I decided to be my own attorney, knowing that it could be nothing against me. I thought I'd let them have it all their own way, and did not ask any questions. When the court went into session, I was asked if I objected to having the witnesses remain in the courtroom during the trial, and I replied that it was immaterial to me who remained in the courtroom. All the witnesses then remained inside, and I noted that there was a steady stream of "messengers" going back and forth between the witnesses and the county attorney during the whole trial, delivering their messages in a whisper. When the trial commenced, there were first some witnesses of little importance, but then a man came up that made me sit up and take notice. He put up his hand and swore that he positively recognized me and that he had seen me in the Morrison store in the afternoon of the same day that Morrison was shot. I did not say anything, but I thought something. This man was a tall, lean man with a thin pale face, black hair and eyes, and a very conspicuous black shiny mustache. I don't know his name and have never been able to find out. (Keep this man in mind, please.) The little boy, Merlin Morrison, was the next witness that attracted my attention. He was the first one to come up and look at me in the morning of the day after my arrest. Being only a little boy, he spoke his mind right out in my presence, and this is what he said: "No, that is not the man at all. The ones I saw were shorter and heavier set."

When he testified at the preliminary hearing, I asked him if he did not make that statement, but he then denied it. I accidentally found a description of the bandit in a newspaper, however, and the description says that the bandit was 5 feet 9 inches tall and weighed about 155 pounds. That description seems to tally pretty well with Merlin Morrison's statement, "The ones I saw were shorter and heavier set." My own height is six feet and I am of a slender built.

The next witness of importance was Mrs. Phoebe Seeley. She said she was coming home from the Empress Theater with her husband and she met two men in a back street in the vicinity of Morrison's store. One of them had "small features and light bushy hair." This description did not suit the county attorney, so he helped her along a little by saying, "You mean medium colored hair like Mr. Hillstrom's, don't you?" After leading her along that way for a while, he asked her this question: "Is the general appearance of Mr. Hillstrom anything like the man you saw?" She answered, "No, I won't, I can't say that."

This is the very same woman who at the district court proved to be the star witness for the prosecution. She did not only describe me into the smallest details, but she also told the jury that the man she saw had scars on both sides of his face, on his nose, and on his neck. I have such scars on my face, and that was practically the testimony that convicted me. Just think of it, a woman not knowing a thing about the murder passing a man in a back street in the dead of a winter night, and six months later she described that man to the smallest details, hat and the cut and color of clothes, height and built, color of eyes and hair, and a number of scars, and when asked, "Is the appearance of Mr. Hillstrom anything like the man you saw?" she answered, "No, I won't, I can't say that." Her husband who was with her was not even there to testify. It is true that the prosecuting attorney put his questions in such a way that all she had to say was "yes, sir" and "all the same, sir," but she said that just the same. With a hostile judge and attorneys, who merely acted as assistant prosecuting attorney, the prosecuting attorney had what in the parlance of the street would be called "easy sailing."

The next witness was Mr. Zeese, detective. When I was sick in bed at the Eselius house in Murray, the lady gave me a red bandana handkerchief to blow my nose on. At the trial she told that she had several dozen bandana handkerchiefs that were used by her boys and brothers when they worked in the smelter. After my arrest Mr. Zeese went to the Eselius house looking for clues. He found this handkerchief, and with his keen, eagle eyes he soon discovered some "creases at the corners." With the intelligence of a super-man he then easily drew the conclusion that this handkerchief had been used for a mask by some "bandit." Then he capped the climax by going on the stand and telling his marvellous discovery to the judge. Mr. Zeese is well known in Salt Lake City, and comments are unnecessary.

The next witness at the preliminary hearing, Mrs. Vera Hanson, said she saw two or three men outside of the Morrison store shortly after the shooting. She heard one of the men exclaim "Bob," or "Oh Bob," and she thought that my voice sounded the same as the voice she heard on the street. I then asked Mrs. Hanson this question: "Do you mean to tell me that you, through that single word Bob, were able to recognize my voice?" Now I am coming to the point.

After the preliminary hearing I got a record of the hearings and took it to my cell in the county jail. I immediately discovered that it had been tampered with, that everything I had said had been misconstrued in a malicious way. It was a little hard to prove it at first but on page 47, I found the question I had put to Mrs. Vera Hanson, and the tampering was so clumsy that a little child could see it. In the records the question reads like this, "Do you mean to tell me that you through the single word (mark, 'single word') 'Oh, Bob, I'm shot,'" four or five words. Here anyone can see that the official court records were altered for the express purpose of "proving" that someone was shot in the Morrison store. I then started to look for testimony of a man with a black shiny mustache but to my great surprise I could not find it anywhere in the records in spite of the fact that this man had positively recognized me at the preliminary hearing. No wonder that this very dignified stenographer, Mr. Rollo, who is also stenographer for the United States Supreme Court, was shaking like a leaf when he put up his hand and swore that the records were "correct" in every detail. The strange part of it is that the supreme court in a statement prepared by them for the press are, so my attorney told me (I am not allowed to see any papers), making the very same mistake. They say that Mrs. Vera Hanson said in her testimony, "Oh, Bob, I'm shot," which is not correct.

At the time when I was shot I was unarmed. I threw my hands up in the air just before the bullet struck me. That accounts for the fact that the bullet hole in my coat is four inches and a half below the bullet hole in my body. The prosecuting attorney endeavors to explain that fact by saying "that the bandit would throw one hand up in surprise when Arlin Morrison got hold of his father's pistol." He also states that the bandit might have been leaning over the counter when he was shot. Very well. If the bandit "threw up his hands in surprise," as he said, that would of course raise the coat some, but it would not raise it four inches and one-half. "Leaning over the counter" would not raise the coat at all. Justice McCarthy agrees with the prosecuting attorney and says that throwing his hands up would be just the very thing that the bandit would do if the boy Arlin made an attempt to shoot him.

Let me ask Mr. McCarthy a question. Suppose that you would some night discover that there was a burglar crawling around in your home then suppose that you would get your gun and surprise that burglar right in the act. If the burglar should then reach for his gun, would you throw up your hands and let the burglar take a shot at you and then shoot the burglar afterward? Or would you shoot the burglar before he had a chance to reach for his gun? Think it over. It is not a question of law but one of human nature. I also wish Mr. McCarthy would try to find it possible to raise a coat on a person four and a half inches in the manner described by the prosecuting attorney.

We will now go back to the bullet. After the bullet had penetrated the bandit, the prosecuting attorney says that it "dropped to the floor" and then disappeared. It left no mark anywhere that an ordinary bullet would. It just disappeared, that's all. Now gentlemen, I don't know a thing about this bullet, but I will say this, that if I should sit down and write a novel, I certainly would have to think up something more realistic than that, otherwise I would never be able to sell it. The story of a bullet that first makes an upshoot of four inches and a half, at an angle of 90 degrees, then cuts around another corner and penetrates a bandit and finally makes a drop like a spit ball and disappears forever, would not be very well received in the twentieth century. And just think of it that the greatest brains in Utah can sit and listen to such rot as that and then say that "Hillstrom" got a fair and impartial trial.

I have heard this case rehashed many times and I wish to state that I have formed my own opinion about this shooting. My opinion is this: Two or three bandits entered the Morrison store for the express purpose of killing Mr. Morrison. As they entered, both of them shouted, "We've got you now!" and started to blaze away with automatic Colt pistols caliber "38," and having the advantage of a surprise, it does not seem reasonable that they would allow a boy to shoot them. The story about that remarkable disappearing bullet; the fact that the official records were changed for the purpose of proving that someone was shot in that store; all that goes to show that there is a decided lack of evidence that anybody was shot in that store outside of the two victims. Nobody saw the Morrison gun fired. Merlin Morrison ran in deadly fright into some back room and hid himself. In spite of the fact that he was almost scared to death he "counted seven shots" and that is supposed to be some more proof that the Morrison gun was discharged. Six shots were fired by the bandits and all the bullets found. But there had to be seven shots fired, otherwise there would be no case against me. The boy "counted seven shots" and that "evidence" is introduced by the state as "proof" that the Morrison gun was discharged. Any sensible person can readily see what chance a frightened boy, or anybody else for that matter, would have to count the shots when two bandits are blazing away with automatic pistols. There were some officers there who claimed that they smelled the end of the gun and that thereby they could tell that the gun had been recently discharged, but the gun expert from the Western Arms Co. exploded that argument. He stated that it was a physical impossibility to determine with any degree of certainty at what time a gun had been discharged, in a case where smokeless powder is used, on account of the fact that the odor of powder is always there. Then there was that empty chamber in the Morrison gun. An officer testified that it was customary for police officers to keep an empty chamber under the hammer of their guns. Morrison used to be a sergeant of police, I was told.

Then there was a "pool of blood" found two or three blocks away from the Morrison store and the prosecution made a whole ocean out of it in spite of the fact that the Utah state chemist would not say that it was human blood.

He said that the blood was of "Mammalian origin."

Then there is Miss Mahan, who is supposed to have heard somebody say "I'm shot." At the preliminary hearing she was very uncertain about it. She said she thought she heard somebody say those words but she was not by any means sure about it.

Now, that's all there is, to my knowledge, and I am positively sure that all this so-called evidence which is supposed to prove that the Morrison gun was discharged on the night of Jan. 10, 1914, would not stand the acid test of a capable attorney, such as I am not in a position to get. At the time of my arrest I did not have money enough to employ an attorney. Thinking that there was nothing to my case, and always being willing to try anything once, I decided to "go it" alone and be my own attorney which I did at the preliminary hearing.

A few days after that hearing an attorney by the name of McDougall came to see me at the county jail. He said he was a stranger in town and had heard about my case and would be willing to take the case for nothing. Seeing that that proposition was in perfect harmony with my bankroll, I accepted his offer. I will say for McDougall, though, that he was honest and sincere about it and would no doubt have carried the case to a successful finish if he had not got mixed up with that miserable shyster Mr. Scott. Before my trial, I pointed out the fact that the preliminary records had been altered, but they said that the said record didn't amount to anything anyway, and that it would do no good to make a holler about it.

Then the trial commenced. The first day went by with the usual questioning of jurors. The second day, however, something happened that did not look right to me. There was a jury of eight men entered the courtroom. They had been serving on some other case and came in to deliver their verdict, which was one of "Guilty." Then the court discharged all the jurors and they all started to go home, but then for some reason Judge Ritchie changed his mind and told three of them to come back and go up in the jury box and be examined for my case. I noted that these men were very surprised and that they did not expect to be retained for jury service. I have therefore good reason to believe that they were never subpoenaed for my case, but simply appointed by the court. One of these men, a very old man by the name of Kimball, was later on made "foreman" of the jury. During the course of the trial I was surprised to see that some of the witnesses were telling entirely different stories from the ones told by them at the preliminary hearing and I then asked my attorney why they did not use the records of the preliminary hearing and pin the witnesses down to their former statements. They then told me that the preliminary hearing had nothing to do with the district court hearing and that they did not amount to anything. They did, however, use said record a little, but only for a bluff. After I had watched this ridiculous grand stand play for a while I came to the conclusion that I had to get rid of these attorneys and either conduct the case myself or else get some other attorney. I therefore stood up the first thing in the morning one day and showed them the door. Being the defendant in the case, I naturally thought I should have the right to say who I wanted to represent me, but to my surprise I discovered that the presiding judge had the power to compel me to have these attorneys in spite of all my protests. He ruled that they remain as "friends of the court" and that settled it. Mr. Scott went after one of the state witnesses in a way that convinced me that he really could do good work when he wanted to. After he got through with this witness (Mrs. Seeley) he came up to me and said, "Now then, how did you like that?" I said, "That's good, but why didn't you do some of that before?" "Well—er" he hesitated. "This was the first witness we had marked for cross-examination." If that is not a "dead give-away," then I don't know anything. It will be noted that Mrs. Seeley is one of the best witnesses for the state.

I will now say something about the pistol which I had in my possession when I called at Dr. McHugh's office to have my wound dressed. The pistol was a "Luger" caliber 30, a pistol of German make. I laid my pistol on the table while the doctor dressed my wound and I thought that he would be able to tell it from other pistols on account of its peculiar construction. He said he did not know, however, what kind of pistol mine was. That was an even break, and whenever I get an even break I am not complaining. He did not, like most of the state witnesses, commit perjury, and is therefore in my opinion a gentleman. There was another doctor, however, by the name of Bird, who dropped in while Dr. McHugh was dressing my wound. He only saw the pistol as I put it in my pocket, he said so at the preliminary hearing, but at the district court hearing he came up and deliberately swore that my pistol was exactly the same kind of pistol as the one that Morrison and his son were killed with.

As I said before, my pistol was a "Luger" 30. It was bought less than a month before my arrest in a second hand store on West South Temple street, near the depot. I was brought down there in an automobile by three officers and the record of the sale was found on the books: price, date of sale, and everything just as I had stated. The books did not show what kind of gun it was, however, and as the clerk who had sold it was in Chicago at the time a telegram was sent to him to which he sent this answer: "Remember selling Luger gun at that time. What's the trouble?" I bought the pistol on Dec. 15, 1913, for $16.50. Anybody may go to the store and see the books.

Now, anyone can readily understand that I am not in a position where I could afford to make any false statements. I have stated the facts as I know them in my own simple way. I think I shall be able to convince every fair-minded man and woman who reads these lines that I did not have a fair and impartial trial in spite of what the learned jurists may say to the contrary. Now if you don't like to see perjurers and dignified crooks go unpunished, if you don't like to see human life being sold like a commodity on the market, then give me a hand. I am going to stick to my principles no matter what may come. I am going to have a new trial or die trying.

Yours for Fair Play,
Joseph Hillstrom.

This letter was presented to the Utah Board of Pardons on September 28, 1915, during a hearing primarily devoted to interrogating local Swedes about why they had reached out to the Swedish government to intervene on Hill's behalf. It was published in the *Deseret Evening News* October 4 issue, and in the IWW newspaper *Solidarity* on October 16. In the *News'* version Hill describes Mrs. Seeley as "one of the last witnesses for the state"; *Solidarity* used "best." The original letter appears not to have survived; however, Seeley testified on the second of four days of the prosecution's presentation, suggesting that *Solidarity* had it right. —AB

Foner: On September 18, Hill and his attorneys, Hilton and Christensen, had appeared before the Utah Board of Pardons. Hill guaranteed the Board that, if granted a new trial, he would be able "to prove absolutely my innocence and to send four or five perjurers to the penitentiary where they belong." Following the hearing, the Board unanimously agreed to deny Joe Hill's plea. Hill was scheduled to be executed on October 1; the defense campaign grew more intense. Pressured by the labor movement of Sweden and by thousands of Swedes in the US, the Swedish government asked Minister Wilhelm Ekengren (its representative to Washington) to investigate the situation. Convinced by his investigation that Hill had not had a fair trial, Ekengren asked President Wilson to obtain a stay of execution. Others, including Elizabeth Gurley Flynn, also appealed to the president for such action.

President Wilson telegraphed Governor Spry of Utah on September 30 asking for postponement of the execution to allow the Swedish government time to present its case. Governor Spry reluctantly postponed the execution. The Board of Pardons met again on October 16 to consider the case. Hill did not appear before the Board, which ordered a hearing to set a new execution date. At that hearing, the judge refused to allow Hill to make a statement, sentencing him to be shot to death on November 19, 1915.

Prison Warden Arthur Pratt read the September 28 letter and then gave it to Governor Spry, who was to release it to the public. (*Deseret Evening News*, September 28, 1915.) Spry did not carry out his promise and had Hill been executed on October 1, there is little doubt that Hill's letter would never have been made public.

Although Hill insisted that how he was wounded on the night that the Morrisons were murdered was "nobody's business but my own," Dr. Frank McHugh, whom he had visited to have his wound treated, had already thrown light on the matter. "I asked him how he came to be shot," Dr. McHugh related three days after he had treated Hill, "and he told me that he and another fellow had quarreled over a girl and that he had struck the other man, who retaliated by shooting him."

The only point linking Hill to the murders was the fact that he had the misfortune to be shot on the same night that the killings occurred. The identification of Hill as the killer by the state's witnesses was always vague and contradictory, and the prosecution's theory was not supported by the physical evidence.

AB: William Adler, in *The Man Who Never Died*, presents a letter by Hilda Erickson (the woman in question), confirming Hill's account in all respects.

UTAH STATE PRISON
SEPTEMBER 30, 1915

ELIZABETH GURLEY FLYNN
511 E. 134TH ST.
NEW YORK CITY N.Y.

Dear Friend & F.W.

Well Gurley I guess I am off for the great unknown to-morrow morning. I have said that I'd have a trial or die trying. They can kill me, but they can never make me "eat my own crow." I consider my self lucky anyway because I have managed to get some of the facts out, but not all of them by any means. Well I had the pleasure to fight under The Red Flag once, anyway, so I guess I've had my share of the fun. I would like to kiss you Good-bye Gurley, not because you are a girl but because you are the original Rebel Girl. Good Bye.

Yours for the O.B.U.,
Joe Hill

Hill wrote this letter, and all of the September 30 letters, with the belief that he would be executed the next day. —AB

UTAH STATE PRISON
SEPTEMBER 30, 1915

SAM MURRAY
3345 17TH ST.
SAN FRANCISCO, CALIFORNIA

Friend and Fellow Worker:

Well, Sam, I received your letter, but you shouldn't feel so sentimental about it. This dying business is not quite so bad as it is cracked up to be. I have always said "a new trial or die trying," and I'll show that I meant it. I was moved to another cell last night and have an armed guard in front of my cell. I was also given a swell feed for the first time in God knows how long, and that is one of the surest signs.

Well, Sam, you and me had a little pleasure at one time that few rebels have had the privilege of having, and I guess I've had my share of the fun after all. Now, just forget me, and say goodbye to the bunch.

Yours for the OBU,
Joe Hill.

P.S. Sent a letter to Caroline.

UTAH STATE PRISON
SEPTEMBER 30, 1915

OSCAR W. LARSON
BOX 148
SANDY, UTAH

Dear comrade—

I have received your welcome letter. The Swedish Consul has told me that you are much trouble in regard to me but you must not be so. I am sure that you understand my position. I have always said that I shall have a new trial because I know that I have the right to one. What has been said has been said. I have said it to my friends, it has been in the papers, and *a man must stand by his word*. I am right, and, as they say in Old Sweden, "I will not budge an inch. I'd rather burst," even though I burst.

Biography do you say? No! We shall not ruin the fine letter paper in writing such trash—the only time that exists for me is the present. I am a "citizen of the world" and I was born on a planet called the Earth. On which side or edge of this planet I first saw the light means so little that it is not worth writing about. The song and the "Girl" that I like the best of my own is "The Rebel Girl" and the one that comes after that as my favorite is "Old Man Noah."

I do not have much to say about my own person. I shall only say that I have always tried to do the little that I could to advance Freedom's Banner a little closer to its goal. I had too one time the great honor of struggling on the battlefield under the Red Flag and I must admit that I am proud of it—I shall now close with an affectionate and comradely greeting to all Swedish revolutionists and Verdantists.

> *I have been and am yours for Freedom and Brotherhood*
> *Joe Hill.*

Hill's letter was written in Swedish and published in *Revolt*, a Swedish progressive paper. "Old Man Noah" was a Swedish song called "Gubben Noak." The Verdantists were members of the Verdandi, the most powerful Swedish organization in America. Larson was president of the Salt Lake City branch.

The words of "Old Man Noah," in English went:
Old man Noah, old man Noah
was a worthy man.
When he left the ark
He planted on the earth,
Old man Noah, old man Noah
was a worthy man.

UTAH STATE PRISON
SEPTEMBER 30, 1915

BEN WILLIAMS
112 HAMILTON AVENUE
CLEVELAND, OHIO
CARE OF *SOLIDARITY*

Dear Friends and F.W.s:

"John Law" has given me his last and final order to get off the earth and stay off. He has told me that many times before, but this time it seems as if he is meaning business. I have said time and again that I was going to get a new trial or die trying. I have told it to my friends. It has been printed in the newspapers, and I don't see why I should "eat my own crow" just because I happen to be up against a firing squad. I have stated my position plainly to everybody, and I won't budge an inch, because I know I am in the right. Tomorrow I expect to take a trip to the planet Mars, and if so, will immediately commence to organize the Mars canal workers into the I.W.W., and we will sing the good old songs so loud that the learned star gazers on earth will once and for all get positive proof that the planet Mars is really inhabited. In the meantime I hope you'll keep the ball a-rolling here. You are on the right track and you are bound to get there. I have nothing to say about myself, only that I have always tried to do what little I could to make this earth a little better for the great producing class, and I can pass off into the great unknown with the pleasure of knowing that I have never in my life, double crossed a man, woman or child.

With a last fond farewell to all true rebels and hearty thanks for the noble support you have given me in this unequal fight, I remain,

Yours for International Solidarity,
Joe Hill

P.S. I have written down for publication, the facts about the case AS I KNOW THEM, I want you to get the truth. Joe.

Ben Williams was the editor of *Solidarity*, which published the letter on October 9, 1915, under the heading: "All the World May Say Here Is a Man."

In his unpublished study, "The Case of Joe Hill," James O. Morris offers this strange comment on this letter: "Hill's mail was subject to prison inspection; perhaps that accounts for the comparatively innocuous, humble tone of his discourse and the reference to a past life free from sin. He may have entertained a remote hope that aroused, official pity might turn back the calendar." (Unpublished manuscript, June 1950, Labadie Collection, University of Michigan Library, p. 97.) Although Morris demonstrates in his study that Joe Hill was the victim of grave injustice and hardly had anything resembling a fair trial, this comment indicates that he does not understand Joe Hill as a person. Hill was not "humble," was proud of his record as a working class fighter, and would never have dreamed of trying to beg for "official pity." Morris demonstrates the same lack of understanding of Hill when he implies that his insistence on a new trial and refusal to plead for commutation of his sentence was due to his desire to "enjoy the distinction of being one of the most principled martyrs in labor history . . . " (ibid, p. 98). Hill's letters make it clear that he believed he was upholding a basic principle of importance to all workers. It will be recalled that he had written to Elizabeth Gurley Flynn: "I have absolutely no desire to be one of them whatye-call-em martyrs. . . ."

UTAH STATE PRISON
OCTOBER 1, 1915

To W.A.F. Ekengren

Wire recd. Have written for publication full statement of facts now in hands of Governor. After you receive and read said statement I am certain you will understand me better. Stay granted until October 16th. Thank you for your noble efforts. I remain yours,

Joseph Hillstrom

Pay no attention to Attorney Scott. Deal with Soren X. Christensen, Salt Lake City, or O. N. Hilton, Denver.

Minister Ekengren had wired Joe Hill on September 30 pleading for him to "give some indication of where and how you received the wound you had dressed the night of the murder or at least won't you indicate where you were."

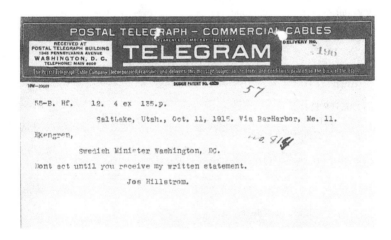

UTAH STATE PRISON
OCTOBER 11, 1915

To W.A.F. Ekengren

Don't act until you receive my written statement.

Jos. Hillstrom.

UTAH STATE PRISON
OCTOBER 14, 1915

To Elizabeth Gurley Flynn

Rec'd the photo of little Buster and all I had to do was to take one glance at it and immediately knew the reason why you felt so homesick when you made your trip to the Pacific Coast. You certainly have a right to be proud of your boy, he's got a forehead like old Shakespeare himself.

Yours for the O.B.U., Joe Hill

P.S. I made "A trip to Honolulu" the other day, and set it to music. It's a March and what's more "It's a Bear." Am sending you same through E.R.

Handwritten music for "A Trip to Honolulu" seems to have survived: Franklin Rosemont found it for his book *Joe Hill: The IWW & the Making of a Revolutionary Workingclass Counterculture* and reproduced the cover, but the lyrics have never been published. —AB

UTAH STATE PRISON
OCTOBER, 1915

TO BUSTER FLYNN
511 E. 134TH ST.
NEW YORK CITY, NEW YORK

To "Bronco Buster" Flynn
Tune. Yankee Doodle.

> I got your picture Buster dear
> A-ridin' on a Pony
> Your pony is a real one too. –
> You wouldn't have a "phony"
>
> CHORUS:
> Buster Flynn he sure is game
> His eyes are full of luster,

I think we'd better change his name
And call him "Bronco Buster"

When you grow up to be a man
Be always "rough and ready"
But never brag about it though
Like windy "Bull Moose Teddy"

And by and by you'll ride out West
Like Cow-boys that you've read of
But don't fall off your pony dear
And break your little head off.

With a Kind Greeting
From Joe Hill

"Bull Moose Teddy" is, of course, Theodore Roosevelt, who had run for president of the United States on the Progressive ("Bull Moose") Party in 1912.

UTAH STATE PRISON
OCTOBER 20, 1915

O. N. HILTON
DENVER, COLORADO

Dear Judge:

Yours at hand. Glad to hear that you had a chance to see the Swedish Minister and have a talk with him. He is getting lots of "explanations" from other sources, I was told. Guess you have heard that my friend Scott has again volunteered his valuable services. I've heard that smallpox is hard to get rid of, but I don't believe it.

Respectfully yrs,
Joseph Hillstrom

P.S. Printed challenge just received. Congratulations. J.H.

Judge Hilton had travelled to Washington at his own expense to discuss the case with Minister Ekengren. "He seems to be wholly convinced that Joe is being railroaded to his death," Hilton wrote to Elizabeth Gurley Flynn after the interview.

Hill was not quite fair to E. B. Scott, his former lawyer. Scott had wired Joseph Tumulty, President Wilson's Secretary, urging the President to intervene, and had written a follow-up letter in which he pointed out that Hill "should never have been found guilty under the evidence." (Both the telegram and the letter are in State Department File 311.582H55 / original through 35, National Archives.)

UTAH STATE PRISON
OCTOBER 27, 1915

O. N. HILTON
DENVER, COLORADO

Dear Judge:

Received your letter of October 23, and in reply will say that I made a mistake in that telegram. I left out the word "I" and that accounts for the misunderstanding. I did not know how the Board decided until the Judge told me in Court. When I found out that it was another death sentence, I stood up and asked for permission to make a statement, but was taken out, and what I had to say was never said, and never will be. Well Judge, I guess the legal part of the case is done now, and I am glad of it. I've had a lawful trial, they say, and as I don't think there is much danger of anybody accepting your challenge, we might well consider the case closed. Now there is only one more thing I'll ask you to do. I know it will be done right when you do it. I would like to have all records of the case sent to Chicago Headquarters, to be kept on file for future references—a copy of the preliminary records; a copy of the District Court records; the two to be kept for comparison; the original of my statement (not copy—Mr. Christensen has the originals). I think Ed Rowan has a copy of the preliminary records, but am not sure of it. I have made some quotations in my statement from the preliminary records, but I wish to see if I made any mistake. If so, you might correct it, and have it typewritten. Now that's all I want done, Judge—you have always kept every promise you made to me, and that's why I want you to do this. In case someone, in the future, should want to learn the details of my case, from beginning to end, I would like to have it all together, and as you are my Attorney, I wish to have it sent from your office. With Best wishes for your Health and Welfare, I remain Respectfully your Client.

Joe Hill

At the end of the session, the Board of Pardons had again denied Hill's application for commutation of sentence and a new trial. On October 18, Hill was again sentenced to be shot—this time on November 19. Surrounded by heavy guards, Hill attempted to address the judge, but was interrupted and rushed back to his cell in the state prison.

The record of the preliminary hearing and the official transcript of the proceedings of the trial over the first thirteen days, including all the evidence introduced against the defendant, has disappeared from the office of the clerk of the Third District Court of Salt Lake City. Volume Two, "Transcript of the witness introduced on behalf of the defendant," including the court's instruction to the jury, is still available in Salt Lake County. The records Hill arranged to have deposited at the Chicago headquarters of the IWW were seized, along with other IWW records, in the postwar raids by the federal government and have disappeared.

UTAH STATE PRISON
OCTOBER, 28 1915

W.A.F. EKENGREN
SWEDISH MINISTER TO THE UNITED STATES

Please send Hilton if finances allow.

UTAH STATE PRISON
NOVEMBER 12, 1915

EKENGREN, SWEDISH MINISTER
WASHINGTON DC

Judge Hilton is the best attorney in the world. Please don't expend any more money on others. The case is closed. Now my friends know I am innocent and I don't care what the rest think. Hearty thanks to you and the whole Swedish nation for your noble support. Remain Yours

Joseph Hillstrom

With the permission of the Swedish government, Minister Ekengren had hired the Salt Lake City legal firm of Pierce, Critchlow and Barrette to look into the case and see if there was anything that could be done to appeal for a further stay of execution, a rehearing before the Board of Pardons, or a new trial. The Salt Lake lawyers reached the conclusion that an appeal to the Supreme Court of the United States was not possible and that nothing further could be done legally for Joe Hill.

UTAH STATE PRISON
NOVEMBER 18, 1915

ELIZABETH GURLEY FLYNN
511 134TH
NEW YORK CITY, NEW YORK

Dear Friend Gurley:

I've been saying Good Bye so much now that it is becoming monotonous but I just can not help to send you a few more lines because you have been more to me than a Fellow Worker. You have been an inspiration and when I composed The Rebel Girl you was right there and helped me all the time. As you furnished the idea I will now that I am gone give you all the credit for that song, and be sure to locate a few more Rebel Girls like yourself, because they are needed and needed badly. I gave Buster's picture to Hilda and she will watch so his pony doesn't run away. With a warm handshake across the continent and a last fond Good-Bye to all I remain yours as ever

Joe Hill

All of the letters dated November 18, 1915, were published in the *Salt Lake Herald-Republican* of November 19, which carried the following item on its first page: "When visited at the state penitentiary yesterday by his attorney, Soren X. Christensen, who broke to him the news that Governor Spry and the board of pardons had refused to accede to President Wilson's request to interfere in his behalf, Hillstrom composed the following messages to be sent to IWW leaders."

UTAH STATE PRISON
NOVEMBER 18, 1915

ELIZABETH GURLEY FLYNN
511 ONE HUNDRED THIRTY-FOURTH STREET
NEW YORK CITY, NEW YORK

Composed new song this week with music, dedicated to the "Dove of Peace." It's coming. And now, good-by, Gurley dear. I have lived like a rebel and I will die like a rebel.

Joe Hill
Salt Lake City Utah
Nov. 18th-1915

The song referred to was "Don't Take My Papa Away From Me." *The Deseret Evening News* of November 19, 1915, described it as "of a sentimental nature and refers to the breaking up of families by war."

NOTE: This was a telegram.

UTAH STATE PRISON
NOVEMBER 18, 1915

W. D. HAYWOOD
CHICAGO, ILLINOIS

Goodbye Bill: I die like a true rebel. Don't waste any time mourning—organize! It is a hundred miles from here to Wyoming. Could you arrange to have my body hauled to the state line to be buried? I don't want to be found dead in Utah.

Joe Hill

Haywood replied to this letter by telegram: "Goodbye, Joe: You will live long in the hearts of the working class. Your songs will be sung wherever the workers toil, urging them to organize."

UTAH STATE PRISON
NOVEMBER 18, 1915

JAMES ROHN
I.W.W. HALL
CEDAR AVENUE
MINNEAPOLIS, MINNESOTA

Wire received. I will die like a rebel. Composed a new song last week. Dedicated to the "Dove of Peace." It's coming your way. My best to everybody. Good-bye.

Joe Hill

James Rohn is undoubtedly James Rowan, IWW organizer.

UTAH STATE PRISON
NOVEMBER 18, 1915

JOHN MAKINS
SAILORS' REST
SAN PEDRO, CALIFORNIA

Your telegram received. Good-bye. Why should I be afraid to die? You will find me the same Joe as in days of yore, in disposition and in ideas. When you get to heaven you will find me on a front seat.

Joe Hill

UTAH STATE PRISON
NOVEMBER 18, 1915

FRISCO LOCAL
3345 SEVENTEENTH STREET
SAN FRANCISCO, CALIFORNIA

Good-by, fellow workers. Forget me and march right on to emancipation.

Joe Hill

MY LAST WILL

My Will is easy to decide
For there is nothing to divide
My kin don't need to fuss and moan
"Moss does not cling to rolling stone."
My body?—Oh!—If I could choose
I would to ashes it reduce
And let the merry breezes blow
My dust to where some flowers grow

Perhaps some fading flower then
Would come to life and bloom again.

This is my Last and Final Will
Good Luck to All of you.

Joe Hill

My Last Will

My Will is easy to decide
For there is nothing to divide
My Kin don't need to fuss and moan
"Moss does not cling to rolling stone"
My body? — Oh. — If I could choose
I would to ashes it reduce
And let the merry breezes blow
My dust to where some flowers grow

Perhaps some fading flower then
Would come to life and bloom again.

This is my Last and Final Will.
Good Luck to All of you

                              Joe Hill

On the last day of his life, Hill was interviewed by a *Salt Lake Herald-Republican* reporter who asked him: "What disposition are you going to make of your effects, your little trinkets, and personal belongings. . . ." Hill replied that he had nothing to dispose of and had never believed in trinkets, keepsakes, and jewelry. "'But I have a will to make, and I'll scribble it. I'll send it to the world in care of Ed Rowan and my I.W.W. friends.' Hillstrom then sat down on the edge of his cot and inscribed the following valedictory to the world."

Then followed the first publication of Joe Hill's famous "Last Will." (*Salt Lake Herald-Republican*, November 18, 1915.)

THE LETTERS OF JOE HILL
BEFORE THE FRAME-UP

NEW YORK CITY
OCTOBER 27, 1902

BEST BROTHER EFRAIM
GOTHENBURG, SWEDEN

The finest Atlantic crossing you can imagine. Singing, music, strolls and food, and food and strolls and music and singing all day long.

Suddenly, while lounging around with some nice English and American women, it's Ulrik right and Ulrik left and that is really funny. Even if the waves are no bigger than in a bigger washbowl. . . .

p.s. Will perform [tonight] at a. . . concert aboard this barge. Duet for violin and piano.

2nd p.s.: I agree with former speaker on all counts. Your brother, James Browning, New York.

Paul and Joel Hägglund

Ulrik is Swedish slang for vomit.

Joel was apparently trying out a new name.

Translated by Rolf Hägglund (Efraim's grandson) for William Adler, who published these excerpts in his *The Man Who Never Died: The Life, Times, and Legacy of Joe Hill, American Labor Icon.* New York, 2011.

SAN FRANCISCO
APRIL 24, 1906

The Catastrophe in San Francisco—A Resident of Gävle Tells the Story

From a former resident of Gävle, Joel Hägglund, who was present at the terrible catastrophe in San Francisco, we received a letter dated the twenty-fourth which gives you some idea of what they had to go through there. He writes among other things:

I woke up on the morning of Wednesday, April 18, at 5:13 by being thrown out of bed. I stood up by grabbing the door handle which I got hold of by accident, and after opening the door, I managed to reach the stairway after much scuffling. How I managed to get down the stairs I really can't tell, but I went fast. I had come half-way down the third and last flight and began to hope I would make it, when suddenly the stairway fell in and I fell straight through the floor down into the basement.

I thought my last moment had come, so I tried to recite one of the old hymns I had learned in Sunday School in Gävle. Then I closed my eyes and waited for my fate.

But then the shakings became weaker and weaker and finally they were completely still. I was pinned between some boards, but managed after some effort to get loose. I moved my arms and legs and found them still working. With the exception of some bruises on my right side and arm, I was completely unhurt. I heard voices and shouts and crept up until I saw a hole large enough for a man to crawl through. In a moment I was out in the street only to meet a sight still worse than was in the basement.

A large six-story house on the other side of the street was flat as a pancake on the ground, and men, women and children were running around in complete disorder. Some had clothing on, some had not more on than a newborn child, and to tell the truth, I wouldn't have taken a walk on main street in the suit I was wearing.

I got hold of a pair of trousers which fit me about as well as a pair of Swedish soldiers' pants, and I went up to an opening where I had a good view of the city. It was a terrible sight to see the large houses, some in ruins, some similar to the leaning tower of Pisa. The ground was full of cracks, some nearly three feet wide, and here and there a dark smoke pillar came out of the ruins, which was the first indication of the terrible fire that later hit San Francisco. It didn't take long before red flames were seen in several places and as all the water pipes had broken and not a drop of water could be had, these spread with terrible speed and the city was changed within a few hours into one single lake of fire.

I saw many moving and heart-rending scenes. Half-naked women carrying small children were driven from their homes. Some refused to leave their old homes, and were seized and bound to keep them from going back into the flames. So-called "martial" law was proclaimed immediately—that means momentary death for the least criminal act of disobedience. Two soldiers came and gave me an axe and put a large steel hat on me, and before I knew what it was all about I was employed as a fireman in the San Francisco Fire Department. I worked for thirty-six hours without food or drink before I was released. My work consisted of helping old people from the fire, carrying out sick from the hospitals, saving valuables, etc. The officer who released me first wrote down my name, then he looked into my pockets for loot. If he had found any, I would have received an extra buttonhole in the vest for all my work and would probably have never written this letter.

Many tried to make money on this calamity and charge senselessly for food. A grocer who sold crackers, small cookies valued about 1/5 of a cent apiece, for ten cents apiece and eggs for two dollars a dozen, made money by the barrels. But then the police were told. They came and gave away all he had to the people outside. Then they brought him out into the street, bound him to a pole and placed a sign over his head with the following inscription: "The man who sold crackers for ten cents apiece. Spit on him." All those who passed spit on him, and I couldn't resist the temptation to go forward and aim at his very long nose. It is hardly necessary here to say that he was a Jew.

My companion, Oscar Westergren, a well-known person from Gävle, I have not seen since the day before the earthquake. I know not whether he is dead or alive, but I am hoping for the best. He may have received some kind of "forced labor."

The fire is not out everywhere and the formerly rich San Francisco is now only a smoking ruin. About a hundred frame houses are all that is left of the "Proud Queen on the Shores of the Pacific Ocean."

Published May 16, 1906, in *Gefle Dågblad*. English translation published in Gibbs M. Smith, *Joe Hill*. Salt Lake City, 1969.

Hill's anti-Semitic remark about the grocer who inflated prices in the wake of the 1906 earthquake hardly seems consistent with the Joe Hill we have come to know. It seems safe to assume that in his travels after the earthquake, and especially after joining the IWW in 1910 (where he would have encountered many Jewish immigrants), that Hill abandoned the notion that Jews were inherently greedy. As his politics developed, he openly ridiculed "Scissor Bills," whose myriad prejudices caused him to comment that if people like that are in heaven, he would prefer to go to hell.

PORTLAND, OREGON (ON THE ROAD)
AUGUST 11, 1910

Another Victim of the Uniformed Thugs

While strolling through the yards at Pendelton, Ore., I saw a fellow sitting on a tie pile. He had his left hand all bandaged up and hanging useless by his side, and the expression on his face was the most hopeless I ever saw. Seeing that he was one of my class I went up and asked him how it happened, and he told me a tale that made the blood boil in my veins. Like many others, he floated into Roseville Junction, Cal., a town noted for murders and bloodshed.

He had a few cents and did not have to beg, but the bull of that town did not like the way he parted his hair, I guess, so he told him to make himself scarce around there. After a bit a train pulled out and he tried to obey orders, but that upholder of law and justice saw him and habitually took a shot at him. His intentions were, of course, the very best, but being a poor shot he only succeeded in crushing the man's hand. The poor fellow might starve to death though, so that blood-thirsty hyena may not get so badly disappointed after all. Not being satisfied with disabling the man for life, he struck him several blows on the head and face with a "sapper" (rubber hose with chunks of lead in the end). Then he threw him in the "tank" without any medical aid whatever, although the hand was bleeding badly. The next morning about 5 o'clock he got a couple of kicks for breakfast and told that if he dared to show his face around there again it would be the grave yard for him. He told me he could not sleep much because the hand was aching all the time and he wished he could get it cut off, because it was no good anyway. Now, fellow workers, how long are those hired murderers, whose chief delight it is to see human blood flowing in streams, going to slaughter and maim our class. There is only one way to stop it—only one remedy—to unite on the industrial field.

Yours,

Joe Hill

Portland Local, No. 92

Published in the August 27, 1910, *Industrial Worker*. This was probably Hill's first contribution to the IWW press.

FROM COALINGA (CALIFORNIA)
JANUARY 12, 1911

I have been working here for a couple of weeks on a building. Wages fair ($3 for 8 hours common labor), but "hash" and "slops" are away out of reach. There will be some street work here after New Years, but I would not advise anybody to come over here unless they've got something rattling in their pockets!

Yours for freedom, HILL, L.U. No. 92

Published in the *Industrial Worker*, January 12, 1911.

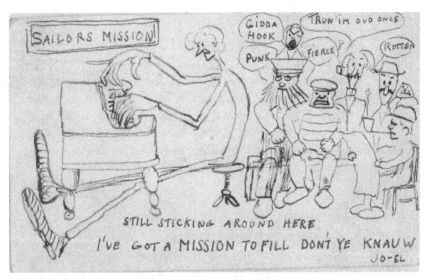

SAN PEDRO, CALIFORNIA
APRIL 29, 1911
Postcard sent to "Charles Rudberg, Sailor's Union Hall, East Street, Frisco, Cal."

SAN PEDRO, CALIFORNIA
MAY 13, 1911

MR. PAUL HEDLUND
ALBION, PA

Well Paul!

I'm off for Mexico to fight with the rebels. I'll see you in heaven if not before.
Adios Hermano.

This is straight goods. Joel.

Postcard to Paul Hedlund (Hill's brother) who moved to Western Pennsylvania. The
postcard included a drawing of Hill wearing a sombrero, shouting "Viva Revolución"
with bullets whizzing by him.

SAN PEDRO, CALIFORNIA
MAY 25, 1911

Vote Right

"I see by the papers" that some smart jink in New York has invented a new voting machine. Guess the working class will break their legs to get the first crack at the "box." But after they have tried all the different brands they might find out that the only "machine" worth while is the one which the capitalists use on us when we ask for more bread for ourselves and our families. The one that works with a trigger. All aboard for Mexico!

Joe Hill, San Pedro

Published in the *Industrial Worker*. Hill ended up fleeing Mexico in mid-June after Mexican troops crushed the Magonista rebellion.

SAN PEDRO, CALIFORNIA
SEPTEMBER 2, 1911

The song of Mauser bullets may be exciting and the rattle of machine guns may also have its trills—but Oh you Hoboeing.

Sent to "Charles Rudberg, Sailor's Union Hall, East Street, Frisco, Cal."

SAN PEDRO, CALIFORNIA
AUGUST 1, 1912

San Pedro Dockworkers Call Strike Off

The strike of the San Pedro Dockworkers is declared off as far as the staying away from work is concerned, but the I. W. W. has 27 different ways of striking and after we have tried the remaining 26 varieties the Stevedore Companies may be willing to grant our demands.

We pulled out about 600 men, including sympathizing non-members, and the tie-up would have been complete had it not been for 10 or 12 my-country-'tis-of-thee stiffs with sick wives, and lots to pay installments on, and other similar excuses. They are strongly in favor of an increase in wages, but when it comes to fighting for it—Oh No! Nothing doing!

When the Stevedore Companies found that they were unable to unload their boats in San Pedro they took them over to Redondo (a port 15 miles from here), where they unloaded by Mexican section hands "borrowed" from the Southern Pacific R.R. Co. The Mexicans were fed on board the vessels and guarded by the strong arm of the law.

Our old friend Otis of the Los Angeles *Crimes* did all he could to advertise the strike and devoted about two columns of fiction and pictures every day to spread the news. We also wish to extend our thanks to the editor of the San Pedro *Daily Nuisance* for his valuable services. In our opinion said editor is only wasting his time printing a 2 by 4 sheet like the *Daily Nuisance*. A man with his imagination and utter disregard for the truth would surely make a hit as a lawyer or Diamond Dick novel writer.

Oscar Jansen, a fellow worker, got 50 days and $100 fine, and two Italian fellow workers were fined $25 each by a corporation controlled judge by the name of Cheesebug for the crime of walking along the wharfs owned by the S.P. Co. Today a young Swede was arrested for looking for a job on the docks. He can hardly speak English and never heard of the I. W. W., but the cops would not believe it and told him to "beat it out of town." It just goes to show how afraid the masters are of "strike-tactic No. 2."

In the meantime Local No. 245 is holding rousing street meetings every night and taking in new members right along and the sentiment for the ONE BIG UNION is growing stronger each day.   —*San Pedro Press Committee*

Published in the *Industrial Worker*, August 15, 1912.

LOCATION UNKNOWN (LIKELY FRESNO)
FEBRUARY 1913

THE PEOPLE
by J. Hill

"The People's flag is deepest red." Who are the people?

"God knows" Taft stands for "the people." If you don't believe it just read the "Los Angeles Crimes" and you will find out that, next to General Debility Otis, Taft is the greatest man in the country. Yes, Fatty stands for the people all right—when he is standing, but he is sitting down most of the time.

And "Teddy da Roos," who used to peddle the Bull Moose, is also very strong for "the people." Some time ago he wasn't so strong and then it was that he invented a policeman's riot club filled with spikes. It would crush the skull of a wage slave with one blow. Yes, "Teddy da Roos," he is strong for "the people."

And Woodhead Wilson, he is for "the people," too. This is what he said in one of his speeches: "Why shouldn't the children of the workingclass be taught to do the work their parents are now doing?" Of course, he meant to say "Why shouldn't the children of the rich be taught to rob the class their parents are now robbing?" And he is going to give "the people" free silver, he says, but if a working stiff wants any silver he has to peel off his coat and hop to the stormy end of a No. 2.

When the Red Flag was flying in Lower California there were not any of "the people" in the ranks of the rebels. Common working stiffs and cow-punchers were in the majority, with a little sprinkling of "outlaws," whatever that is.

"The people" used to come down there on Sunday in their stinkwagons to take a look at "The wild men with their Red Flag" for two-bits a look. But if the Mexican or the Indian regiment happened to be a little overjoyed from drinking "mescal" and took a notion to have a bit of sociable target practice, or to try to make buttonholes for one another without taking their clothes off, then "the people" would almost break their legs to get to their stinkwagons and make a bee-line for the "Land of the Graft and the Home of the Slave."

Well, it is about time that every rebel wakes up to the fact that "the people" and the workingclass have nothing in common. Let us sing after this "The Workers' flag is deepest red" and to hell with "the people."

Published in the *Industrial Worker*, February 20, 1913.

⤞ SONGS, POEMS, AND COMICS ⤝
IN CHRONOLOGICAL ORDER

TWO VICTIMS OF SOCIETY

He can't afford to have a home.   She never had a chance.   That's why they are both selling themselves to the highest bidder.

Published in the January 26, 1911, *Industrial Worker.*

DER CHIEF, OF FRESNO

Who is the freak that had the cheek,
The crawling, slimy, cringing sneak,
That prohibits us the right to speak?
    Der Chief.

Who gave the workers the loud Ha! Ha!
Who tried to trample down the law?
Who handed us the deal so raw?
    Der Chief.

Who is the most notorious liar?
Who had stool pigeons in his hire?
Who mobbed our speakers, camp did fire?
    Der Chief.

Who is this grey-haired guy so wise?
Who winks and blinks his bleary eyes?
Thinks he has the workers hypnotized?
    Der Chief.

Who was the czar with haughty frown?
Who gave us floaters out of town?
And was surprised when we turned him down?
>Der Chief.

Who recommended the cat-o'-nine
And wished to have it soaked in brine,
To make the workers fall in line?
>Der Chief.

Who said the working men were scum?
That we were tramps and on the bum?
And that he had us on the run?
>Der Chief.

Who was the despot who used his might?
Who broke the backbone of our fight?
Vagged all our leaders in one night?
>Der Chief.

Who wears that worried look of pain,
When he finds the fight is on again?
Leaders coming on every train.
>Der Chief.

Who is the mutt with shiny pate,
Who tried to chase us from this state,
And is surely going to meet his fate?
>Der Chief.

Hill's command of English slang and idioms really comes through in this chant, published in the February 2, 1911, *Industrial Worker*. It was written to mock Fresno's police chief, William Shaw, during the IWW's Free Speech Fights.

The January 5, 1911, *Industrial Worker* included a report from Christmas Eve of the jailed soapboxers stopping a three-day hunger strike. They were given dry bedding and clothes, replacing those that had been drenched by the fire department who turned their hoses on protesters. Two prisoners had decided to take a "floater out of town": they plead guilty on vagrancy charges in exchange for a promise to leave the city. The union declared themselves victor in March when the court acquitted Frank Little, who stood trial on behalf of nearly a hundred arrested Wobblies, jailed for weeks for violating made-up ordinances.

THE PREACHER AND THE SLAVE

Long-haired preachers come out every night,
Try to tell you what's wrong and what's right;
But when asked how 'bout something to eat
They will answer with voices so sweet:

> *CHORUS:*
> *You will eat, bye and bye,*
> *In that glorious land above the sky;*
> *Work and pray, live on hay,*
> *You'll get pie in the sky when you die.*

The starvation army they play,
They sing and they clap and they pray
'Till they get all your coin on the drum
Then they'll tell you when you're on the bum: *[CHORUS]*

Holy Rollers and jumpers come out,
They holler, they jump and they shout.
"Give your money to Jesus," they say,
"He will cure all diseases today."   *[CHORUS]*

If you fight hard for children and wife—
Try to get something good in this life—
You're a sinner and bad man, they tell,
When you die you will sure go to hell.   *[CHORUS]*

Workingmen of all countries, unite,
Side by side we for freedom will fight!
When the world and its wealth we have gained
To the grafters we'll sing this refrain:

> *FINAL CHORUS:*
> *You will eat, bye and bye,*
> *When you've learned how to cook and to fry.*
> *Chop some wood, 'twill do you good,*
> *And you'll eat in the sweet bye and bye.*

Tune: "Sweet By and By" (S. Fillmore Bennett and J. P. Webster)
First published in the 1911 edition of the IWW's Little Red Songbook, but either

misattributed (the author credited was F. B. Brechler) or Hill was trying out a pseudonym that didn't last long. This iconic song, which added the phrase "Pie in the Sky" to the American vernacular, was written to ridicule anti-labor clergy, in particular the Salvation Army.

CASEY JONES—THE UNION SCAB

The workers on the S. P. line to strike sent out a call;
But Casey Jones, the engineer, he wouldn't strike at all;
His boiler it was leaking, and its drivers on the bum,
And his engine and its bearings, they were all out of plumb.

> *Casey Jones kept his junk pile running;*
> *Casey Jones was working double time;*
> *Casey Jones got a wooden medal,*
> *For being good and faithful on the S. P. line.*

The workers said to Casey: "Won't you help us win this strike?"
But Casey said: "Let me alone, you'd better take a hike."
Then some one put a bunch of railroad ties across the track,
And Casey hit the river bottom with an awful crack.

> *Casey Jones hit the river bottom;*
> *Casey Jones broke his blessed spine;*
> *Casey Jones was an Angelino,*
> *He took a trip to heaven on the S. P. line.*

When Casey Jones got up to heaven, to the Pearly Gate,
He said: "I'm Casey Jones, the guy that pulled the S. P. freight."
"You're just the man," said Peter, "our musicians went on strike;
You can get a job a'scabbing any time you like."

> *Casey Jones got a job in heaven;*
> *Casey Jones was doing mighty fine;*
> *Casey Jones went scabbing on the angels,*
> *Just like he did to workers of the S. P. line.*

The angels got together, and they said it wasn't fair,
For Casey Jones to go around a'scabbing everywhere.
The Angels' Union No. 23, they sure were there,
And they promptly fired Casey down the Golden Stairs.

Casey Jones went to Hell a'flying;
"Casey Jones," the Devil said, "Oh fine:
Casey Jones, get busy shovelling sulphur;
That's what you get for scabbing on the S. P. Line."

Tune: "The Ballad of Casey Jones" (Wallace Saunders)
Written in support of a strike by 35,000 railroad workers that was undercut (and ultimately defeated in 1915) by union scabbing. The January 19, 1911, *Industrial Worker* reported:

> Result of Craft, Scabby Unionism: The wages of section men on the Southern Pacific Line have been cut from $1.60 to $1.25 per day. The section men are Mexicans and they have gone on strike against the cut. The misery among strikers makes a horrible story of hunger and cold, sick children, and women with babies with no beds or clothing. The engineers have lately had a raise of pay, and the railroad companies don't intend to be the losers. The engineers believe in identity of interests and openly avow that they will scab on others if they strike, so long as they get what they are after. Nice Unionism.

The song was first published in 1911 as a card sold to support the strike fund; also published in the 1912 and subsequent editions of the Little Red Songbook.

JOHN GOLDEN AND THE LAWRENCE STRIKE

In Lawrence, when the starving masses struck for more to eat
And wooden-headed Wood tried the strikers to defeat,
To Sammy Gompers wrote and asked him what he thought,
And this is just the answer that the mailman brought:

> *CHORUS:*
> *A little talk—*
> *A little talk with Golden*
> *Makes it all right, all right;*
> *He'll settle any strike,*
> *If there's coin enough in sight;*
> *Just take him up to dine*
> *And everything is fine—*
> *A little talk with Golden*
> *Makes it right, all right.*

The preachers, cops and money-kings were working hand in hand,
The boys in blue, with stars and stripes were sent by Uncle Sam;

Still things were looking blue 'cause every striker knew
That weaving cloth with bayonets is hard to do.

John Golden had with Mr. Wood a private interview,
He told him how to bust up the "I double double U."
He came out in a while and wore the Golden smile.
He said: "I've got all labor leaders skinned a mile."

John Golden pulled a bogus strike with all his "pinks and stools."
He thought the rest would follow like a bunch of crazy fools.
But to his great surprise the "foreigners" were wise,
In one big solid union they were organized.

> *FINAL CHORUS:*
> *That's one time Golden did not*
> *Make it right, all right;*
> *In spite of all his schemes*
> *The strikers won the fight.*
> *When all the workers stand*
> *United hand in hand,*
> *The world with all its wealth*
> *Shall be at their command.*

Tune: "A Little Talk with Jesus"
Written for the Lawrence, Massachusetts, textile strike which began in January 1911, known as the "Bread and Roses" strike. John Golden was the president of the United Textile Workers, an AFL-affiliated union which tried to settle with the bosses for less than strikers were demanding. Samuel Gompers was the president of the AFL and this would not be his last mention in Hill's songs. The song was first published in the 1912 edition of the Little Red Songbook.

WHERE THE FRASER RIVER FLOWS

Fellow workers pay attention to what I'm going to mention,
For it is the fixed intention of the Workers of the World.
And I hope you'll all be ready, true-hearted, brave and steady,
To gather 'round our standard when the red flag is unfurled.

> *CHORUS:*
> *Where the Fraser River flows, each fellow worker knows,*
> *They have bullied and oppressed us, but still our union grows.*

And we're going to find a way, boys, for shorter hours and better pay, boys
And we're going to win the day, boys, where the river Fraser flows.

For these gunny-sack contractors have all been dirty actors,
And they're not our benefactors, each fellow worker knows.
So we've got to stick together in fine or dirty weather,
And we will show no white feather, where the Fraser River flows.   *[CHORUS]*

Now the boss the law is stretching, bulls and pimps he's fetching,
And they are a fine collection, as Jesus only knows.
But why their mothers reared them, and why the devil spared them,
Are questions we can't answer, where the Fraser River flows.

Tune: "Where the River Shannon Flows" (James I. Russell)
First published in the 1912 edition of the Little Red Songbook. The Fraser River
strike of railroad construction workers began in March 1912.

MARTIN WELCH AND STUART

Martin Welch is mad as hell and don't know what to do.
And all his gunnysack contractors are feeling mighty blue.
For we have tied their railroad line and scabs refuse to come,
And we will keep on striking till we put them on the bum.
Till we put them on the bum, till we put them on the bum,
And we will keep on striking till we put them on the bum.

Tune: "Wearing of the Green" (trad.)
This is an unpublished song, as recalled by Fraser River "camp delegate" Louis
Moreau. Moreau relayed his recollections of Hill to Fred Thompson, an active Wob-
bly who served five years in prison on criminal syndicalism charges and served as
General Secretary-Treasurer.

WE WON'T BUILD NO MORE RAILROADS FOR OVERALLS AND SNUFF

We have got to stick together, boys,
And fight with all our might.
It's a case of no surrender
We have got to win this fight.
From these gunnysack contractors,
We will take no more bluff;
And we won't build no more railroads

For our overalls and snuff.
For our overalls and snuff, for our overalls and snuff,
We won't build no more railroads
For our overalls and snuff.

Tune: "Wearing of the Green" (trad.)
Unpublished song, as recalled by Louis Moreau.

SKOOKUM RYAN THE WALKING BOSS

Skookum Ryan the Walking Boss
Came tearing down the line,
Says he, "You dirty loafers take your coats off
Or go and get your time."

Unpublished song, as recalled by Louis Moreau, who said this "very popular" song had five or six stanzas. This is the only one to survive.

LET BILL DO IT

Hey, all you girls and fellows
That do depend on Bill
To do your work and duties,
I'll put you next, I will.
I'll put you next to Billy,
I've known him since the 'Quake;
Of all the Weary Willies,
That guy, he takes the cake.
He is so gol durn lazy
He wouldn't do a tap'
I rather would depend on
Some fool Missouri yap.
Now take my tip, you workers
That slave in mine and mill,
And never do depend upon
That good for nothing Bill.

This poem about Hill's frustration with workers who rely on lazy bureaucrats was published in the *Industrial Worker*, October 10, 1912. Underneath the title appeared, in parentheses: "Written by J. Hill, and dedicated to those who have nothing to lose but their *chairs*."

COFFEE AN'

An employment shark the other day I went to see,
And he said come in and buy a job from me,
Just a couple of dollars, for the office fee,
The job is steady and the fare is free.

> *CHORUS:*
> *Count your pennies, count them, count them one by one,*
> *Then you plainly see how you are done,*
> *Count your pennies, take them in your hand,*
> *Sneak into a Jap's and get your coffee an'.*

I shipped out and worked and slept in lousy bunks,
And the grub it stunk as bad as forty-'leven skunks,
When I slaved a week the boss he said one day,
You're too tired, you are fired, go and get your pay.

When the clerk commenced to count, Oh holy gee!
Road, school and poll tax and hospital fee.
Then I fainted, and I nearly lost my sense
When the clerk he said: "You owe me fifty cents."

When I got back to town with blisters on my feet,
There I heard a fellow speaking on the street.
And he said: "It is the workers' own mistake.
If they stick together they get all they make."

And he said: "Come in and join our union grand.
Who will be a member of this fighting band?"
"Write me out a card," says I, "By Gee!
The Industrial Worker is the dope for me."

> *FINAL CHORUS:*
> *Count your workers, count them, count them one by one,*
> *Join our union and we'll show you how it's done.*
> *Stand together, workers, hand in hand,*
> *Then you will never have to live on coffee an'.*

Tune: "Count Your Blessings" (Johnson Ottman/E. O. Excell)
First published in the 1912 edition of the Little Red Songbook.

MR. BLOCK

Please give me your attention, I'll introduce to you
A man that is a credit to "Our Red, White, and Blue,"
His head is made of lumber, and solid as a rock;
He is a common worker and his name is Mr. Block.
And Block he thinks he may
Be president some day.

> CHORUS:
> Oh Mr. Block, you were born by mistake,
> You take the cake, you make me ache.
> Tie a rock on your block and then jump in the lake,
> Kindly do that for Liberty's sake.

Yes, Mr. Block is lucky; he found a job, by gee!
The sharks got seven dollars, for job and fare and fee.
They shipped him to a desert and dumped him with his truck,
But when he tried to find his job, he sure was out of luck,
He shouted, "That's too raw,
I'll fix them with the law." *[CHORUS]*

Block hiked back to the city, but wasn't doing well.
He said "I'll join the union—the great A. F. of L."
He got a job next morning, got fired in the night,
He said, "I'll see Sam Gompers and he'll fix that foreman right."
Sam Gompers said, "You see,
You've got our sympathy." *[CHORUS]*

Election day he shouted, "A Socialist for Mayor!"
The "comrade" got elected, he happy was for fair,
But after the election he got an awful shock,
A great big socialistic Bull did rap him on the block.
And Comrade Block did sob,
"I helped him to his job." *[CHORUS]*

The money kings in Cuba blew up the gunboat Maine,
But Block got awful angry and blamed it all on Spain.
He went right in the battle and there he lost his leg.
And now he's peddling shoestrings and is walking on a peg. *[CHORUS]*

He shouts, "Remember Maine,
Hurrah! To hell with Spain!" *[CHORUS]*

Poor Block he died one evening, I'm very glad to state,
He climbed the golden ladder up to the pearly gate.
He said, "Oh Mister Peter, one word I'd like to tell,
I'd like to meet the Astorbilts and John D Rockefell."
Old Pete said, "Is that so?
You'll meet them down below." *[CHORUS]*

Tune: "It Looks Like a Big Night Tonight" (Harry Williams and Egbert Van Alstyne)
This song was inspired by a popular and long-running comic series by Ernest Riebe published in the IWW press beginning in November 1912. Riebe was a master at depicting his character Block's ironic "bad luck," which stemmed from his blind belief in church, state, and other variants of authority. Hill accurately captured the spirit of the comics in his song. The "Mr. Block" song was first published in the January 23, 1913, *Industrial Worker* and made its Little Red Songbook debut in the fifth edition, released March 1913.

EVERYBODY'S JOINING IT

Fellow workers, can't you hear,
There is something in the air.
Everywhere you walk everybody talks
'Bout the I. W. W.
They have got a way to strike
That the master doesn't like—
Everybody sticks,
That's the only trick,
All are joining now.

> *CHORUS:*
> *Everybody's joining it, joining what? Joining it!*
> *Everybody's joining it, joining what? Joining it!*
> *One Big Union, that's the workers' choice,*
> *One Big Union, that's the only choice,*
> *One Big Union, that's the only noise,*
> *One Big Union, shout with all your voice;*
> *Make a noise, make a noise, make a noise, boys,*

Everybody's joining it, joining what? Joining it!
Everybody's joining it, joining what? Joining it!
Joining in this union grand,
Boys and girls in every land;
All the workers hand in hand—
Everybody's joining it now.

The Boss is feeling mighty blue,
He don't know just what to do.
We have got his goat, got him by the throat,
Soon he'll work or go starving.
Join I. W. W.,
Don't let bosses trouble you,
Come and join with us—
Everybody does—
You've got nothing to lose.   *[CHORUS]*

Will the One Big Union Grow?
Mister Bonehead wants to know.
Well! What do you think, of that funny gink,
Asking such foolish questions?
Will it grow? Well! Look a here,
Brand new locals everywhere,
Better take a hunch,
Join the fighting bunch,
Fight for Freedom and Right.   *[CHORUS]*

Tune: "Everybody's Doin' It" (Irving Berlin)
First published in the 1913 edition of the Little Red Songbook.

SCISSOR BILL

You may ramble 'round the country anywhere you will,
You'll always run across that same old Scissor Bill.
He's found upon the desert, he is on the hill,
He's found in every mining camp and lumber mill.
He looks just like a human, he can eat and walk,
But you will find he isn't, when he starts to talk.
He'll say, "This is my country," with an honest face,

While all the cops they chase him out of every place.

> CHORUS:
> Scissor Bill, he's a little dippy,
> Scissor Bill, he has a funny face.
> Scissor Bill, should drown in Mississippi,
> He is the missing link that Darwin tried to trace.

And Scissor Bill he couldn't live without the booze,
He sits around all day and spits tobacco juice.
He takes a deck of cards and tries to beat the Chink!
Yes, Bill would be a smart guy if he only could think.
And Scissor Bill he says: "This country must be freed
From Niggers, Japs and Dutchmen and the gol durn Swede."
He says that every cop would be a native son
If it wasn't for the Irishman, the sonna fur gun.

> CHORUS:
> Scissor Bill, the "foreigners" is cussin',
> Scissor Bill, he says: "I hate a Coon";
> Scissor Bill, is down on everybody,
> The Hottentots, the bushmen and the man in the moon.

Don't try to talk your union dope to Scissor Bill,
He says he never organized and never will.
He always will be satisfied until he's dead,
With coffee and a doughnut and a lousy old bed.
And Bill, he says he gets rewarded thousand fold,
When he gets up to Heaven on the streets of gold.
But I don't care who knows it, and right here I'll tell,
If Scissor Bill is goin' to Heaven, I'll go to Hell.

> CHORUS:
> Scissor Bill, he wouldn't join the union,
> Scissor Bill, he says, "Not me, by Heck!"
> Scissor Bill, gets his reward in Heaven,
> Oh! sure. He'll get it, but he'll get it in the neck.

Tune: "Steamboat Bill" (Ren Shields and the Leighton Brothers)
A scissorbill is an unclass-conscious worker who would cut off his own nose, or

"bill," to spite his face. Mocking the racist and anti-immigrant words uttered by so many scissorbills, this song was first published in the February 16, 1913, *Industrial Worker*. However, it's very difficult to imagine that this song would have been embraced by the IWW's Asian and African American members. The inclusion of abusive epithets in an attempt to ridicule those who uttered them must have come off as ham-handed and uncomfortable when it was first written. This song appears in the March 1913 and subsequent editions of the Little Red Songbook, sometimes editing out the scissorbill-ian words. —AB

WE WILL SING ONE SONG

We will sing one song of the meek and humble slave,
The horn-handed son of the soil,
He's toiling hard from the cradle to the grave,
But his master reaps the profits from his toil.
Then we'll sing one song of the greedy master class,
They're vagrants in broadcloth, indeed,
They live by robbing the ever-toiling mass,
Human blood they spill to satisfy their greed.

> *CHORUS:*
> *Organize! Oh, toilers, come organize your might;*
> *Then we'll sing one song of the workers' commonwealth,*
> *Full of beauty, full of love and health.*

We will sing one song of the politician sly,
He's talking of changing the laws;
Election day all the drinks and smokes he'll buy,
While he's living from the sweat of your brow.
Then we'll sing one song of the girl below the line,
She's scorned and despised everywhere,
While in their mansions the "keepers" wine and dine
From the profits that immoral traffic bear. *[CHORUS]*

We will sing one song of the preacher, fat and sleek,
He tells you of homes in the sky.
He says, "Be generous, be lowly, and be meek,
If you don't you'll sure get roasted when you die."
Then we sing one song of the poor and ragged tramp,
He carries his home on his back;

Too old to work, he's not wanted 'round the camp,
So he wanders without aim along the track.   *[CHORUS]*

We will sing one song of the children in the mills,
They're taken from playgrounds and schools,
In tender years made to go the pace that kills,
In the sweatshops, 'mong the looms and the spools.
Then we'll sing one song of the One Big Union Grand,
The hope of the toiler and slave,
It's coming fast; it is sweeping sea and land,
To the terror of the grafter and the knave.   *[CHORUS]*

Tune: "My Old Kentucky Home" (Stephen Foster)
First published in the March 6, 1913, *Industrial Worker*; appears in the March 1913
and subsequent editions of the Little Red Songbook.

WHAT WE WANT

We want all the workers in the world to organize
Into a great big union grand
And when we all united stand
The world for workers we demand
If the working class could only see and realize
What mighty power labor has
Then the exploiting master class
It would soon fade away.

> *CHORUS:*
> *Come all ye toilers that work for wages,*
> *Come from every land,*
> *Join the fighting band,*
> *In one union grand,*
> *Then for the workers we'll make upon this earth a paradise*
> *When the slaves get wise and organiʒe.*

We want the sailor and the tailor and the lumberjacks,
And all the cooks and laundry girls,
We want the guy that dives for pearls,
The pretty maid that's making curls,
And the baker and staker and the chimneysweep,

97

We want the man that's slinging hash,
The child that works for little cash
In one union grand.   *[CHORUS]*

We want the tinner and the skinner and the chamber-maid,
We want the man that spikes on soles,
We want the man that's digging holes,
We want the man that's climbing poles,
And the trucker and the mucker and the hired man,
And all the factory girls and clerks,
Yes, we want every one that works,
In one union grand.   *[CHORUS]*

Tune: "Rainbow" (Percy Wenrich and Alfred Bryan)
First published in the March 27, 1913, *Industrial Worker*.

SHOULD I EVER BE A SOLDIER

We're spending billions every year
For guns and ammunition.
"Our Army" and "our Navy" dear,
To keep in good condition;
While millions live in misery
And millions died before us,
Don't sing "My Country 'tis of thee,"
But sing this little chorus.

> *CHORUS:*
> *Should I ever be a soldier,*
> *'Neath the Red Flag I would fight;*
> *Should the gun I ever shoulder,*
> *It's to crush the tyrant's might.*
> *Join the army of the toilers,*
> *Men and women fall in line,*
> *Wage slave of the world! Arouse!*
> *Do your duty for the cause,*
> *For Land and Liberty.*

And many a maiden, pure and fair,
Her love and pride must offer

On Mammon's altar in despair,
To fill the master's coffer.

The gold that pays the mighty fleet,
From tender youth he squeezes,
While brawny men must walk the street
And face the wintry breezes.   *[CHORUS]*

Why do they mount their gatling gun
A thousand miles from ocean,
Where hostile fleet could never run—
Ain't that a funny notion?
If you don't know the reason why,
Just strike for better wages,
And then, my friends—if you don't die—
You'll sing this song for ages.   *[CHORUS]*

Tune: "Colleen Bawn" (Ed Madden and J. Fred Helf)
First published in the April 3, 1913, *Industrial Worker* and appears in the March 1913 and subsequent editions of the Little Red Songbook.

THE TRAMP

If you all will shut your trap,
I will tell you 'bout a chap,
That was broke and up against it, too, for fair
He was not the kind that shirk,
He was looking hard for work,
But he heard the same old story everywhere:

> *CHORUS:*
> *Tramp, tramp, tramp, keep on a-tramping,*
> *Nothing doing here for you;*
> *If I catch you 'round again,*
> *You will wear the ball and chain,*
> *Keep on tramping, that's the best thing you can do.*

He walked up and down the street,
'Till the shoes fell off his feet,
In a house he spied a lady cooking stew,
And he said, "How do you do,

May I chop some wood for you?"
What the lady told him made him feel so blue: *[CHORUS]*

'Cross the street a sign he read,
"Work for Jesus," so it said,
And he said, "Here is my chance, I'll surely try,"
And he kneeled upon the floor,
'Till his knees got rather sore,
But at eating-time he heard the preacher cry: *[CHORUS]*

Down the street he met a cop,
And the copper made him stop,
And he asked him, "When did you blow into town?
Come with me up to the judge."
But the judge he said, "Oh, fudge,
Bums that have no money needn't come around."   *[CHORUS]*

Finally came that happy day
When his life did pass away,
He was sure he'd go to heaven when he died,
When he reached the pearly gate,
Saint Peter, mean old skate,
Slammed the gate right in his face and loudly cried: *[CHORUS]*

In despair he went to Hell,
With the Devil for to dwell,
For the reason he'd no other place to go.
And he said, "I'm full of sin,
So for Christ's sake, let me in!"
But the Devil said, "Oh, beat it! You're a 'bo!"   *[CHORUS]*

Tune: "Tramp! Tramp! Tramp!" (George F. Root)
Hill deftly reworked a Civil War tune penned to lift the spirits of Union Army prisoners of war and, invoking the sound of their marching, turned it into a song about hard-up hoboes, keeping the best part of the refrain intact. The original tune was so catchy that others besides Hill repurposed it. Preacher Clare Herbert Woolston used it as the basis of "Jesus Loves the Little Children." Hill's last verse about our tramp even being refused entry into hell was not always included when the song was printed. First published in the March 1913 edition of the Little Red Songbook

and later in the May 22, 1913, *Industrial Worker*.

DOWN IN THE OLD DARK MILL

How well I do remember
That mill along the way,
Where she and I were working
For fifty cents a day.
She was my little sweetheart;
I met her in the mill—
It's a long time since I saw her.
But I love her still.

> *CHORUS:*
> *Down in the Old Black Mill,*
> *That's where first we met.*
> *Oh! that loving thrill*
> *I shall ne'er forget;*
> *And those dreamy eyes,*
> *Blue like summer skies.*
> *She was fifteen—*
> *My pretty queen—*
> *In the Old Black Mill.*

We had agreed to marry
When she'd be sweet sixteen.
But then—one day I crushed it—
My arm in the machine.
I lost my job forever—
I am a tramp disgraced.
My sweetheart still is slaving
In the same old place.   *[CHORUS]*

Tune: "Down By the Old Mill Stream" (Tell Taylor)
First published in the March 1913 edition of the Little Red Songbook.

THE GIRL QUESTION

A little girl was working in a big department store,
Her little wage for food was spent; her dress was old and tore.

She asked the foreman for a raise, so humbly and so shy,
And this is what the foreman did reply:

> *CHORUS:*
> *Why don't you get a beau?*
> *Some nice old man, you know!*
> *He'll give you money if you treat him right.*
> *If he has lots of gold,*
> *Don't mind if he is old.*
> *Go! Get some nice old gentleman tonight.*

The little girl then went to see the owner of the store,
She told the story that he'd heard so many times before.
The owner cried: "You are discharged! Oh, my, that big disgrace,
A ragged thing like you around my place!"   *[CHORUS]*

The little girl she said: "I know a man that can't be wrong,
I'll go and see the preacher in the church where I belong."
She told him she was down and out and had no place to stay.
And this is what the holy man did say: *[CHORUS]*

Next day while walking round she saw a sign inside a hall,
It read: The One Big Union Will Give Liberty to All.
She said: I'll join that union, and I'll surely do my best,
And now she's gaily singing with the rest:

> *FINAL CHORUS:*
> *Oh, Workers do unite!*
> *To crush the tyrant's might,*
> *The One Big Union Banner is Unfurled—*
> *Come slaves from every land,*
> *Come join this fighting band,*
> *It's named Industrial Workers of the World.*

Tune: "Tell Mother I'll Be There" (Charles M. Fillmore)
First published in the March 1913 edition of the Little Red Songbook.

NEARER MY JOB TO THEE

Nearer my job to thee,
Nearer with glee,

Three plunks for the office fee,
But my fare is free.
My train is running fast,
I've got a job at last,
Nearer my job to thee
Nearer to thee.

Arrived where my job should be,
Nothing in sight I see,
Nothing but sand, by gee,
Job went up a tree.
No place to eat or sleep,
Snakes in the sage brush creep.
Nero a saint would be,
Shark, compared to thee.

Nearer to town! each day
(Hiked all the way),
Nearer that agency,
Where I paid my fee,
And when that shark I see
You'll bet your boots that he
Nearer his god shall be.
Leave that to me.

Tune: "Nearer My God to Thee" (Lowell Mason)
First published in the March 1913 edition of the Little Red Songbook.

STUNG RIGHT

When I was hiking 'round the town to find a job one day,
I saw a sign: "A thousand men are wanted right away,"
To take a trip around the world in Uncle Sammy's fleet,
I signed my name a dozen times upon a great big sheet.

> *CHORUS:*
> *I was stung right, stung right, S-T-U-N-G,*
> *Stung right, stung right, E. Z. Mark, that's me*
> *When my term is over, and again I'm free,*
> *There'll be no more trips around the world for me.*

The man he said, "The U. S. Fleet, that is no place for slaves,
The only thing you have to do is stand and watch the waves."
But in the morning, five o'clock, they woke me from my snooze,
To scrub the deck and polish brass, and shine the captain's shoes. *[CHORUS]*

One day a dude in uniform to me commenced to shout,
I simply plugged him in the jaw, and knocked him down and out;
They slammed me right in irons then and said, "You are a case."
On bread and water then I lived for twenty-seven days. *[CHORUS]*

One day the captain said, "Today I'll show you something nice,
All hands line up, we'll go ashore and have some exercise."
He made us run for seven miles as fast as we could run,
And with a packing on our back that weighed a half a ton. *[CHORUS]*

Some time ago when Uncle Sam he had a war with Spain,
And many of the boys in blue were in the battle slain,
Not all were killed by bullets, though; no, not by any means,
The biggest part that died were killed by Armour's Pork and Beans. *[CHORUS]*

Tune: "Sunlight, Sunlight" (W. S. Weeden)
First published in the March 1913 Little Red Songbook. Also appears in the May 29, 1913, *Industrial Worker.*

THERE IS POWER IN A UNION

Would you have freedom from wage slavery,
Then join in the grand Industrial band;
Would you from mis'ry and hunger be free,
Then come! Do your share, like a man.

> *CHORUS:*
> *There is pow'r, there is pow'r*
> *In a band of workingmen.*
> *When they stand hand in hand,*
> *That's a pow'r, that's a pow'r*
> *That must rule in every land—*
> *One Industrial Union Grand.*

Would you have mansions of gold in the sky,
And live in a shack, way in the back?
Would you have wings up in heaven to fly,
And starve here with rags on your back?   *[CHORUS]*

If you've had "nuff" of "the blood of the lamb,"
Then join in the grand Industrial band;
If, for a change, you would have eggs and ham.
Then come! Do your share, like a man.   *[CHORUS]*

If you like sluggers to beat off your head,
Then don't organize, all unions despise,
If you want nothing before you are dead,
Shake hands with your boss and look wise.   *[CHORUS]*

Come, all ye workers, from every land,
Come join in the grand Industrial band.
Then we our share of this earth shall demand.
Come on! Do your share, like a man.   *[CHORUS]*

Tune: "There Is Power in the Blood"
First published in the March 1913 edition of the Little Red Songbook.

THE WHITE SLAVE

One little girl, fair as a pearl,
Worked every day in a laundry;
All that she made for food she paid,
So she slept on a park bench so soundly;
An old procuress spied her there,
And whispered softly in her ear:

> *CHORUS:*
> *Come with me now, my girly,*
> *Don't sleep out in the cold;*
> *Your face and tresses curly*
> *Will bring you fame and gold,*
> *Automobiles to ride in, diamonds and silks to wear,*
> *You'll be a star bright, down in the red light,*
> *You'll make your fortune there.*

Same little girl, no more a pearl,
Walks all alone 'long the river,
Five years have flown, her health is gone,
She would look at the water and shiver,
Whene'er she'd stop to rest and sleep,
She'd hear a voice call from the deep: *[CHORUS]*

Girls in this way, fall every day,
And have been falling for ages,
Who is to blame? You know his name,
It's the boss that pays starvation wages.
A homeless girl can always hear
Temptations calling everywhere.   *[CHORUS]*

CONSTITUTIONAL GUARANTEE:–LIFE? LIBERTY? AND THE PURSUIT OF--A JOB!

Tune: "Meet Me Tonight In Dreamland" (Leo Friedman)
First published in the March 1913 edition of the Little Red Songbook and also appears in the April 10, 1913, *Industrial Worker*.
Published in the April 24, 1913, *Industrial Worker*.

THE OLD TOILER'S MESSAGE

"Darling I am growing old"—
So the toiler told his wife—
"Father Time the days have tolled
Of my usefulness in life.
Just tonight my master told me
He can't use me any more.
Oh, my darling, do not scold me,
When the wolf comes to our door."

> *CHORUS:*
> *To the scrap heap we are going*
> *When we're overworked and old—*
> *When our weary heads are showing*
> *Silver threads among the gold.*

"Darling, I am growing old"—
He once more his wife did tell—
"All my labor pow'r I've sold
I have nothing more to sell.
Though I'm dying from starvation
I shall shout with all my might
To the coming generation.
I shall shout with all my might"— *[CHORUS]*

Tune: "Silver Threads Among the Gold" (Hart Pease Danks)
First published in an August 1913 songbook released by the Seattle IWW.

THE REBEL'S TOAST

If Freedom's road seems rough and hard,
And strewn with rocks and thorns,
Then put your wooden shoes on, pard,
And you won't hurt your corns.
To organize and teach, no doubt,
Is very good—that's true,
But still we can't succeed without
The Good Old Wooden Shoe.

Published in *Solidarity* on June 27, 1914, which happens to be the same day Hill was convicted of murder. Its first Little Red Songbook appearance was in the December 1914 edition. Wooden shoes were used by the IWW as a symbol of sabotage, the word itself derived from the French *sabot*. The etymology of sabotage has always been a matter of debate. Here, Hill is clearly advocating putting *on* wooden shoes to slow the work, protect the worker, and win demands.

TA-RA-RA BOOM DE-AY

I had a job once threshing wheat, worked sixteen hours with hands and feet.
And when the moon was shining bright, they kept me working all the night.
One moonlight night, I hate to tell, I "accidentally" slipped and fell.
My pitchfork went right in between some cog wheels of that thresh-machine.

> *Ta-ra-ra-boom-de-ay!*
> *It made a noise that way.*
> *And wheels and bolts and hay,*
> *Went flying every way.*
> *That stingy rube said, "Well!*
> *A thousand gone to hell."*
> *But I did sleep that night,*
> *I needed it all right.*

Next day that stingy rube did say, "I'll bring my eggs to town today;
You grease my wagon up, you mutt, and don't forget to screw the nut."
I greased his wagon all right, but I plumb forgot to screw the nut,
And when he started on that trip, the wheel slipped off and broke his hip.

> *Ta-ra-ra-boom-de-ay!*
> *It made a noise that way,*
> *That rube was sure a sight,*
> *And mad enough to fight;*
> *His whiskers and his legs*
> *Were full of scrambled eggs;*
> *I told him, "That's too bad—*
> *I'm feeling very sad."*

And then that farmer said, "You turk! I bet you are an I-Won't-Work."
He paid me off right there, By Gum! So I went home and told my chum.
Next day when threshing did commence, my chum was Johnny on the fence;

And 'pon my word, that awkward kid, he dropped his pitchfork, like I did.

> *Ta-ra-ra-boom-de-ay!*
> *It made a noise that way,*
> *And part of that machine*
> *Hit Reuben on the bean.*
> *He cried, "Oh me, oh my;*
> *I nearly lost my eye."*
> *My partner said, "You're right—*
> *It's bedtime now, good night."*

But still that rube was pretty wise, these things did open up his eyes.
He said, "There must be something wrong; I think I work my men too long."
He cut the hours and raised the pay, gave ham and eggs for every day,
Now gets his men from union hall, and has no "accidents" at all.

> *Ta-ra-ra-boom-de-ay!*
> *That rube is feeling gay;*
> *He learned his lesson quick,*
> *Just through a simple trick.*
> *For fixing rotten jobs*
> *And fixing greedy slobs,*
> *This is the only way,*
> *Ta-ra-ra-boom-de-ay!*

Tune: "Ta-Ra-Ra Boom De-Ay" (attributed to Henry Sayers) (1891)
First published in the March 1916 Joe Hill Memorial Edition of the Little Red Songbook, but probably written at some point before Hill was arrested.

Police found the following three romantic songs in Hill's room after when they shot him in his sleep and arrested him in January 1914. The IWW never published them, and Hill kept the subject(s) of his affection to himself. It's not clear if Hill had music in mind for any of these songs, but musician Bucky Halker gave his own tunes to "Aeroplane" and "Dreamland Girl" to honor a seldom-seen, lovestruck side of Hill on the centenary of his execution.

COME AND TAKE A JOY-RIDE IN MY AEROPLANE

If you will be my sweetheart, I'll take you for a ride
Among the silv'ry clouds up in the sky.
Then, far away from sorrows like eagles we will glide,
And no one will be there but you and I.
Say, darling, if you'll be my little honey dove,
We'll fly above and coo and love.
I'll take you from this dusty earth to where the air
Is pure and crystal clear—and there
I'll give my promise to be true,
While gliding 'mong the silv'ry clouds with you.

Come and take a joy-ride in my aeroplane tonight,
Way beyond the clouds, where all the stars are shining bright.
There I'd like to look into your loving eyes of blue,
And if I should fall, then I know I'd fall in love with you.

If you will be my sweetheart, I'll take you to the stars,
The man in the moon will meet you face to face.
We'll take a trip to Venus, to Jupiter and to Mars,
And with the comets we will run a race.
We'll go to the milky way, where all the milk is sold
In cups of gold, so I was told.
Our little honeymooning trip shall be a scream,
A sweet and lovely dream.
Come, put your little head close to my heart,
And promise that we'll never, never part.

MY DREAMLAND GIRL

Would you like to get acquainted with my Dreamland Girl divine?
Never was a picture painted fairer than this girl of mine.
Sweet and graceful like a pansy, bright and charming like a pearl,
She's the idol of my fancy, she's my own—my Dreamland Girl.

Charming Fairy Queen of my dreams,
Ever before me your face brightly beams:
Night and day I'm dreaming of you,
Some day my sweet dreams perhaps will come true.

She is coy and captivating, Venus-like in grace and pose,
With an air more fascinating than the fragrance of the Rose.
Like the stars her eyes are shining 'neath a wealth of golden hair,
And my heart is ever pining for my Dreamland Girl so fair.

OH, PLEASE LET ME DANCE THIS WALTZ WITH YOU

When I hear that melody, with its rhythmic harmony,
Then I feel just like I'd be in a dream entrancing,
And I'd like to float through space, softly glide from place to place,
With the fascinating grace of a fairy dancing.

Oh, please let me dance this waltz with you,
And look in your dreamy eyes of blue.
Sweet imagination, smooth, gliding sensation,
Oh, love, I would die just for dancing this waltz with you.

Listen to that mellow strain, come and let us waltz again.
Please don't let me ask in vain; I just feel like flying,
Put your head close to my heart, And we'll never, never part.
Come my darling, let us start, from joy I'm nearly dying.

Next page: A fake front page of "*Class War News,*" a nonexistent publication. Joe Hill created this comic about IWW submarines. It was published in the IWW publication *Industrial Solidarity,* October 24, 1914.

CLASS WAR NEWS

I. W. W. Submarines Are Annoying The Enemy Everywhere

WORKERS OF THE WORLD AWAKEN!

Workers of the world, awaken!
Break your chains, demand your rights.
All the wealth you make is taken
By exploiting parasites.
Shall you kneel in deep submission
From your cradles to your graves?
Is the height of your ambition
To be good and willing slaves?

> *CHORUS:*
> *Arise, ye prisoners of starvation!*
> *Fight for your own emancipation;*
> *Arise, ye slaves of every nation.*
> *In One Union grand.*
> *Our little ones for bread are crying,*
> *And millions are from hunger dying;*
> *The end the means is justifying,*
> *'Tis the final stand.*

If the workers take a notion,
They can stop all speeding trains;
Every ship upon the ocean
They can tie with mighty chains.
Every wheel in the creation,
Every mine and every mill,
Fleets and armies of the nation,
Will at their command stand still.   *[CHORUS]*

Join the union, fellow workers,
Men and women, side by side;
We will crush the greedy shirkers
Like a sweeping, surging tide;
For united we are standing,
But divided we will fall;
Let this be our understanding—
"All for one and one for all."   *[CHORUS]*

Workers of the world, awaken!
Rise in all your splendid might;
Take the wealth that you are making,
It belongs to you by right.
No one will for bread be crying,
We'll have freedom, love and health.
When the grand red flag is flying
In the Workers' Commonwealth.   *[CHORUS]*

Words and music written by Joe Hill in the Salt Lake City prison. Published in *Solidarity*, September 1914, this was probably Hill's first song composed in prison. It was printed with an announcement that henceforth all orders for the Little Red Songbook would include an insert on Joe Hill's case. In this way, "the songs, of which he has contributed so many, will be a medium of arousing the workers in his behalf." Subsequently issued as sheet music and in the March 1916 Joe Hill Memorial Edition of the Little Red Songbook.

IT'S A LONG WAY DOWN TO THE SOUPLINE

Bill Brown was just a working man like others of his kind.
He lost his job and tramped the streets when work was hard to find.
The landlord put him on the stem, the bankers kept his dough,
And Bill heard everybody sing, no matter where he'd go:

> *CHORUS:*
> *It's a long way down to the soupline,*
> *It's a long way to go.*
> *It's a long way down to the soupline,*
> *And the soup is thin I know.*
> *Good bye, good old pork chops,*
> *Farewell, beefsteak rare;*
> *It's a long way down to the soupline,*
> *But my soup is there.*

So Bill and sixteen million men responded to the call
To force the hours of labor down and thus make jobs for all.
They picketed the industries and won the four-hour day
And organized a General Strike so men don't have to say: *[CHORUS]*

The workers own the factories now, where jobs were once destroyed

114

By big machines that filled the world with hungry unemployed.
They all own homes, they're living well, they're happy, free and strong,
But millionaires wear overalls and sing this little song: *[CHORUS]*

Tune: "It's a Long, Long Way to Tipperary" (Harry Williams)
Discussed in Hill's letters to Sam Murray of December 2, 1914; February 5, 1915;
March 22, 1915; and to Elizabeth Gurley Flynn on February 19, 1915, this song
was commissioned by Murray, who needed to send Hill the original music as he
was unfamiliar with the tune. First published as a card with proceeds going to Hill's
defense fund, and then in the 25th edition of the Little Red Songbook in 1933.

This comic, drawn by Hill and published posthumously in the *One Big Union Monthly*
in November 1919, might have been inspired by the IWW's unemployed workers
organizing in New York City.

THE REBEL GIRL

There are women of many descriptions
In this queer world, as everyone knows.
Some are living in beautiful mansions,
And are wearing the finest of clothes.

There are blue-blooded queens and princesses,
Who have charms made of diamonds and pearl;
But the only and thoroughbred lady
Is the Rebel Girl.

> CHORUS:
> *That's the Rebel Girl, that's the Rebel Girl!*
> *To the working class she's a precious pearl.*
> *She brings courage, pride and joy*
> *To the fighting Rebel Boy.*
> *We've had girls before, but we need some more*
> *In the Industrial Workers of the World.*
> *For it's great to fight for freedom*
> *With a Rebel Girl.*

Yes, her hands may be hardened from labor,
And her dress may not be very fine;
But a heart in her bosom is beating
That is true to her class and her kind.
And the grafters in terror are trembling
When her spite and defiance she'll hurl;
For the only and thoroughbred lady
Is the Rebel Girl.   *[CHORUS]*

Hill discussed his work on "Rebel Girl" in letters to Sam Murray on February 13, 1914, and Katie Phar on February 16 and May 7, 1915. He referred to Elizabeth Gurley Flynn as a Rebel Girl on July 15, 1915. The song was published as sheet music by the IWW and in the 1916 edition of the Little Red Songbook.

DON'T TAKE MY PAPA AWAY FROM ME

A little girl with her father stayed, in a cabin across the sea,
Her mother dear in the cold grave lay; with her father she'd always be—
But then one day the great war broke out and the father was told to go;
The little girl pleaded—her father she needed.
She begged, cried and pleaded so:

> CHORUS:
> *Don't take my papa away from me, don't leave me there all alone.*

He has cared for me so tenderly, ever since mother was gone.
Nobody ever like him can be, no one can so with me play.
Don't take my papa away from me; please don't take papa away.

Her tender pleadings were all in vain, and her father went to the war.
He'll never kiss her good night again, for he fell 'mid the cannon's roar.
Greater a soldier was never born, but his brave heart was pierced one day;
And as he was dying, he heard some one crying,
A girl's voice from far away: *[CHORUS]*

Words and music written by Hill in the Salt Lake County Jail on the eve of his execution, and referenced in his November 18, 1915, letter to Elizabeth Gurley Flynn. First published in the 1916 Joe Hill Memorial Edition of the Little Red Songbook.

Mr. Highbrow: "These wars are terrible. Here they have shot a hole in this 2,000-year old painting."
Mrs. Highbrow: "Oh! Horrors! How thoughtless of that commander not to order some peasants to stand in front of it during the battle."

Published posthumously in the *One Big Union Monthly*, November 1919.

117

SOURCES

by Philip Foner

The letters to Sam Murray were first published in the December 1923 *Industrial Pioneer* under the title, "The Last Letters of Joe Hill." All of the letters to Elizabeth Gurley Flynn were in the possession of Miss Flynn, and I wish to express my gratitude to her for permission to reprint them. Her death as this book was being prepared was a great loss to the American people and especially the American working class, which she so ably and selflessly served for most of her long life. The letters to Katie Phar and Gus (January 3, 1915) are in the Wallace Stegner Collection in the Hoover Institution on War, Revolution and Peace Library, Stanford University, and I wish to thank Mr. Stegner for permission to reprint them. The letter to the Editor of *Solidarity*, November 29, 1914, the letters to Ed Rowan, July 14 and 22, 1915, the letters to O. N. Hilton, July 14, October 20, 1915, the letters to William D. Haywood, July 28, November 18, 1915, were published in *Solidarity*. The letter to Ben Williams, September 30, 1915, was published in *Solidarity* and the *Deseret Evening News*. The letter to the Editor of the *Salt Lake Telegram* was published in that paper. Part of the letter appeared in the *International Socialist Review*, vol. 16, October 1915, pp. 222–23. The letter to Oscar W. Larson was published in *Revolt* December 1915. A copy of this issue of the magazine which was published in Swedish is in the "Joe Hill File Box," Labadie Collection, University Library, University of Michigan, and I wish to thank Edward Weber, curator of the Labadie Collection, for furnishing me with a reproduction. The letter to the Utah Board of Pardons was published in *Solidarity* and the *Deseret Evening News*. A copy of the letter to O. N. Hilton, October 27, 1915, was in the possession of Elizabeth Gurley Flynn. "My Last Will" was first published in the *Salt Lake Herald-Republican*, as were all the letters dated November 18, 1915.

The telegrams of October 1 and November 12, 1915, to Swedish Minister Ekengren are in the archives of the Royal Ministry for Foreign Affairs in Stockholm, and I wish to thank Wilhelm Carlgren, Head of Archives, for furnishing me with copies.

ON THE EXPANDED EDITION

by Alexis Buss

There have been many significant developments in our understanding of Joe Hill since Philip Foner brought out the first edition of *The Letters of Joe Hill* in 1965.

Biographies by Gibbs Smith and William Adler have given us a much better understanding of Joe Hill's life before Salt Lake City police tried to kill him in his bed and then framed him for murder. We now know that Hill was not only a gifted and prolific songwriter, but that he was deeply involved in the life of his union, the Industrial Workers of the World, and that he was an active member of the Gävle Workers Federation before emigrating to the United States. Hill joined free speech fights, spoke on behalf of the IWW at a San Francisco rally supporting the San Diego free speech fighters (who faced police and vigilante terror so extreme that the state government was finally forced to take notice), served as secretary of the San Pedro dockworkers strike committee, and traveled to British Columbia to lend a hand in the Fraser River strike, writing songs to bolster morale on the thousand-mile picket line. He joined an IWW battalion that fought alongside the Magonistas in the Mexican Revolution. He was in Utah not simply because he was looking for work after he had been blacklisted for his role in the San Pedro strike, but also because the IWW was actively organizing in the region and he wanted to lend a hand.

We also now have a pretty good idea of who murdered the Morrisons (a career criminal who police had in custody but released when they decided to frame Joe Hill), and of how Hill got shot. We know, in short, that Hill was a lifelong rebel, and that this fact played a central role in the decision to try and execute him for a crime the authorities knew full well he had not committed.

Archivists were only beginning to collect documents on radical movements when the first edition was compiled, and so, as Dr. Foner explains in his note on sources, he relied primarily upon personal collections—especially that of Elizabeth Gurley Flynn, who played a key role in defense efforts—and published letters. Since then, many additional letters have come to light as their recipients donated them to archives, government archives have been opened, and researchers have located scattered records.

This collection adds six prison letters and telegrams (and the complete texts of two letters to Katie Phar that were excerpted in the original), several drawings (some originally sent as postcards), and letters and other writings

119

dating from Joe Hill's arrival in the United States in 1902 through his move to Utah in 1913. I have also expanded the notes, for those less familiar with IWW history and Hill's case.

This collection is certainly not complete. Hill often refers to other letters that appear not to have survived. There are no known surviving letters from his first eight months in captivity, and only correspondence with his family and with one friend survives from before his arrest (in addition to his writings for the IWW press). Nor can we be certain that all of his published writings have been identified, as the *Industrial Worker* published many articles without identifying their author. There are also tantalizing fragments suggesting other work. Archie Green's papers include the cover to a songbook issued by the Los Angeles IWW for which Hill designed the cover. No copies of the songbook itself have been located. In his correspondence Hill mentions having written a new song, "A Trip to Honolulu," for which only the sheet music seems to have survived. And Hill's letters are replete with mentions of other letters that thus far remain undiscovered.

Elizabeth Gurley Flynn's collection, which Dr. Foner reviewed with her by his side, is now located in the Tamiment Library & Robert F. Wagner Labor Archives at New York University. Documents in Sweden at the time of Dr. Foner's original research were given to the Walter P. Reuther Library of Wayne State University in Detroit by King Carl XVI Gustav of Sweden when he visited the library in April 1976. Letters to Katie Phar are in the Rare Book & Manuscript Library of the University of Illinois Library in Urbana. I am particularly indebted to Jon Bekken for his patience and tenacity for ferreting out Joe Hill's writings.

ARCHIVAL SOURCES, BY CORRESPONDENT

Joe Hill's surviving letters are scattered among several archives. Where letters are reprinted from newspapers or other publications, original publication information is noted following the text.

W.A.F. Ekengren: Archives of the Royal Ministry of Foreign Affairs, National Archives, Stockholm, Sweden.

Elizabeth Gurley Flynn: Elizabeth Gurley Flynn Joe Hill Case Papers, box 371, Tamiment Library & Robert F. Wagner Labor Archives, New York University.

Efraim Hägglund: Arbetarrörelsens Arkiv, Stockholm, Sweden.

Paul Hedlund (Hägglund): Archives Collection, Länsmuseet Gävleborg, Gävle, Sweden.

O. N. Hilton: Elizabeth Gurley Flynn Joe Hill Case Papers, box 371, Tamiment Library & Robert F. Wagner Labor Archives, New York University.

Sam Murray: Archives Collection, Länsmuseet Gävleborg, Gävle, Sweden; Llano del Rio Collection, box 2, folder 1, Dept. of Manuscripts, Henry E. Huntington Library, San Marino, CA (Feb. 13, June 6, Aug. 12, Sept. 30, 1915).

Katie Phar: University of Illinois at Urbana-Champaign Library, Archives, Baskette Collection, box 13.

Ed Rowan: Elizabeth Gurley Flynn Joe Hill Case Papers, box 371, Tamiment Library & Robert F. Wagner Labor Archives, New York University.

Charles Rudberg: Archives of Labor & Urban Affairs, Wayne State University, Detroit, MI.

E. W. Vanderleith: General Correspondence, box 2 (folder August 1915), Frank P. Walsh Papers, Special Collections, Manuscripts and Archives Division, New York Public Library.

ABOUT THE AUTHORS

Joe Hill (1879–1915) was a Swedish American labor activist, songwriter, and member of the Industrial Workers of the World. At Joe Hill's funeral procession in Chicago, 30,000 people marched, and a news reporter asked: "What kind of man is this whose death is celebrated with songs of revolt, and who has at his bier more mourners than any prince or potentate?" Joe Hill's letters answer this question.

Philip S. Foner (1910–1994) was one of the most prominent Marxist historians in the United States. A prolific author and editor, he tirelessly documented the lives of workers, African Americans, and political radicals.

Alexis Buss served six terms as General Secretary-Treasurer of the Industrial Workers of the World and also worked as a union organizer specializing in direct action strategies. She has coedited the Solidarity Forever Labor History Calendar since 1998 and is the author of *The Union on Our Own Terms*, drawn from columns she wrote on solidarity unionism for the *Industrial Worker* for nearly a decade.

ABOUT HAYMARKET BOOKS

Haymarket Books is a nonprofit, progressive book distributor and publisher, a project of the Center for Economic Research and Social Change. We believe that activists need to take ideas, history, and politics into the many struggles for social justice today. Learning the lessons of past victories, as well as defeats, can arm a new generation of fighters for a better world. As Karl Marx said, "The philosophers have merely interpreted the world; the point however is to change it."

We take inspiration and courage from our namesakes, the Haymarket Martyrs, who gave their lives fighting for a better world. Their 1886 struggle for the eight-hour day, which gave us May Day, the international workers' holiday, reminds workers around the world that ordinary people can organize and struggle for their own liberation. These struggles continue today across the globe—struggles against oppression, exploitation, hunger, and poverty.

It was August Spies, one of the Martyrs who was targeted for being an immigrant and an anarchist, who predicted the battles being fought to this day. "If you think that by hanging us you can stamp out the labor movement," Spies told the judge, "then hang us. Here you will tread upon a spark, but here, and there, and behind you, and in front of you, and everywhere, the flames will blaze up. It is a subterranean fire. You cannot put it out. The ground is on fire upon which you stand."

We could not succeed in our publishing efforts without the generous financial support of our readers. Many people contribute to our project through the Haymarket Sustainers program, where donors receive free books in return for their monetary support. If you would like to be a part of this program, please contact us at info@haymarketbooks.org.

Order these titles and more online at www.haymarketbooks.org or call 773-583-7884.

ALSO FROM HAYMARKET BOOKS

101 CHANGEMAKERS: REBELS AND RADICALS WHO CHANGED US HISTORY
EDITED BY MICHELE BOLLINGER AND DAO X. TRAN

ALWAYS ON STRIKE: FRANK LITTLE AND THE WESTERN WOBBLIES
ARNOLD SNEAD

THE BENDING CROSS: A BIOGRAPHY OF EUGENE V. DEBS
RAY GINGER, FOREWORD BY MIKE DAVIS

EMMA
HOWARD ZINN

A GREAT AND TERRIBLE WORLD: THE PRE-PRISON LETTERS, 1908–1926
ANTONIO GRAMSCI, EDITED AND TRANSLATED BY DEREK BOOTHMAN

THE LABOR WARS: FROM THE MOLLY MAGUIRES TO THE SIT-DOWNS
SIDNEY LENS

LUCY PARSONS: AN AMERICAN REVOLUTIONARY
CAROLYN ASHBAUGH

THE MEXICAN REVOLUTION: A SHORT HISTORY 1910–1920
STUART EASTERLING

THE OLD MAN: JOHN BROWN AT HARPER'S FERRY
TRUMAN NELSON, INTRODUCTION BY MIKE DAVIS

**RADICAL UNIONISM: THE RISE AND FALL
OF REVOLUTIONARY SYNDICALISM**
RALPH DARLINGTON

RANK AND FILE: PERSONAL HISTORIES BY WORKING-CLASS ORGANIZERS
ALICE LYND AND STAUGHTON LYND

REVOLUTION IN SEATTLE: A MEMOIR
HARVEY O'CONNOR

**SUBTERRANEAN FIRE: A HISTORY OF WORKING-CLASS RADICALISM IN
THE UNITED STATES**
SHARON SMITH

**WAR ON WAR: LENIN, THE ZIMMERWALD LEFT,
AND THE ORIGINS OF COMMUNIST INTERNATIONALISM**
R. CRAIG NATION